2

FOUR CORNERS

Second Edition

Student's Book
with Online Self-Study

JACK C. RICHARDS & DAVID BOHLKE

CAMBRIDGE
UNIVERSITY PRESS

CAMBRIDGE
UNIVERSITY PRESS & ASSESSMENT

Shaftesbury Road, Cambridge CB2 8EA, United Kingdom

One Liberty Plaza, 20th Floor, New York, NY 10006, USA

477 Williamstown Road, Port Melbourne, VIC 3207, Australia

314–321, 3rd Floor, Plot 3, Splendor Forum, Jasola District Centre, New Delhi – 110025, India

103 Penang Road, #05–06/07, Visioncrest Commercial, Singapore 238467

Cambridge University Press & Assessment is a department of the University of Cambridge.

We share the University's mission to contribute to society through the pursuit of education, learning and research at the highest international levels of excellence.

www.cambridge.org
Information on this title: www.cambridge.org/fourcorners

First published 2012
Second edition 2019

20 19 18 17

Printed in Brazil by Forma Certa Grafica Digital LTDA

A catalogue record for this publication is available from the British Library

ISBN 978-1-108-56021-4 Student's Book with Online Self-Study 2
ISBN 978-1-108-57070-1 Student's Book with Online Self-Study 2A
ISBN 978-1-108-62772-6 Student's Book with Online Self-Study 2B
ISBN 978-1-108-62849-5 Student's Book with Online Self-Study and Online Workbook 2
ISBN 978-1-108-57586-7 Student's Book with Online Self-Study and Online Workbook 2A
ISBN 978-1-108-62779-5 Student's Book with Online Self-Study and Online Workbook 2B
ISBN 978-1-108-45958-7 Workbook 2
ISBN 978-1-108-45959-4 Workbook 2A
ISBN 978-1-108-45961-7 Workbook 2B
ISBN 978-1-108-65228-5 Teacher's Edition with Complete Assessment Program 2
ISBN 978-1-108-56039-9 Full Contact with Online Self-Study 2
ISBN 978-1-108-63454-0 Full Contact with Online Self-Study 2A
ISBN 978-1-108-68906-9 Full Contact with Online Self-Study 2B
ISBN 978-1-108-45968-6 Presentation Plus Level 2

Additional resources for this publication at www.cambridge.org/fourcorners

Authors' acknowledgments

Many people contributed to the development of *Four Corners*. The authors and publisher would like to particularly thank the following **reviewers**:

Nele Noe, **Academy for Educational Development, Qatar Independent Secondary School for Girls**, Doha, Qatar; Pablo Stucchi, **Antonio Raimondi School** and **Instituto San Ignacio de Loyola**, Lima, Peru; **Nadeen Katz, Asia University, Tokyo, Japan;** Tim Vandenhoek, **Asia University**, Tokyo, Japan; Celso Frade and Sonia Maria Baccari de Godoy, **Associação Alumni**, São Paulo, Brazil; Rosane Bandeira, **Atlanta Idiomas**, Manaus, Brazil; Cacilda Reis da Silva, **Atlanta Idiomas**, Manaus, Brazil; Gretta Sicsu, **Atlanta Idiomas**, Manaus, Brazil; Naila Maria Cañiso Ferreira, **Atlanta Idiomas**, Manaus, Brazil; Hothnã Moraes de Souza Neto, **Atlanta Idiomas**, Manaus, Brazil; Jacqueline Kurtzious, **Atlanta Idiomas**, Manaus, Brazil; José Menezes Ribeiro Neto, **Atlanta Idiomas**, Manaus, Brazil; Sheila Ribeiro Cordeiro, **Atlanta Idiomas**, Manaus, Brazil; Juliana Fernandes, **Atlanta Idiomas**, Manaus, Brazil; Aline Alexandrina da Silva, **Atlanta Idiomas**, Manaus, Brazil; Kari Miller, **Binational Center**, Quito, Ecuador; Alex K. Oliveira, **Boston University**, Boston, MA, USA; Noriko Furuya, **Bunka Gakuen University**, Tokyo, Japan; Robert Hickling, **Bunka Gakuen University**, Tokyo, Japan; John D. Owen, **Bunka Gakuen University**, Tokyo, Japan; Elisabeth Blom, **Casa Thomas Jefferson**, Brasília, Brazil; Lucilena Oliveira Andrade, **Centro Cultural Brasil Estados Unidos (CCBEU Belém)**, Belém, Brazil; Marcelo Franco Borges, **Centro Cultural Brasil Estados Unidos (CCBEU Belém)**, Belém, Brazil; Geysa de Azevedo Moreira, **Centro Cultural Brasil Estados Unidos (CCBEU Belém)**, Belém, Brazil; Anderson Felipe Barbosa Negrão, **Centro Cultural Brasil Estados Unidos (CCBEU Belém)**, Belém, Brazil; Henry Grant, **CCBEU – Campinas**, Campinas, Brazil; Maria do Rosário, **CCBEU – Franca**, Franca, Brazil; Ane Cibele Palma, **CCBEU Inter Americano**, Curitiba, Brazil; Elen Flavia Penques da Costa, **Centro de Cultura Idiomas – Taubaté**, Taubaté, Brazil; Inara Lúcia Castillo Couto, **CEL LEP – São Paulo**, São Paulo, Brazil; Sonia Patricia Cardoso, **Centro de Idiomas Universidad Manuela Beltrán**, Barrio Cedritos, Colombia; Geraldine Itiago Losada, **Centro Universitario Grupo Sol (Musali)**, Mexico City, Mexico; Nick Hilmers, **DePaul University**, Chicago, IL, USA; Monica L. Montemayor Menchaca, **EDIMSA**, Metepec, Mexico; Angela Whitby, **Edu-Idiomas Language School**, Cholula, Puebla, Mexico; Mary Segovia, **El Monte Rosemead Adult School**, Rosemead, CA, USA; Dr. Deborah Aldred, **ELS Language Centers, Middle East Region**, Abu Dhabi, United Arab Emirates; Leslie Lott, **Embassy CES**, Ft. Lauderdale, FL, USA; M. Martha Lengeling, **Escuela de Idiomas**, Guanajuato, Mexico; Pablo Frias, **Escuela de Idiomas UNAPEC**, Santo Domingo, Dominican Republic; Tracy Vanderhoek, **ESL Language Center**, Toronto, Canada; Kris Vicca and Michael McCollister, **Feng Chia University**, Taichung, Taiwan; Flávia Patricia do Nascimento Martins, **First Idiomas**, Sorocaba, Brazil; Andrea Taylor, **Florida State University in Panama**, Panamá, Panama; Carlos Lizárraga González, **Groupo Educativo Angloamericano**, Mexico City, Mexico; Bo-Kyung Lee, **Hankuk University of Foreign Studies**, Seoul, South Korea; Dr. Martin Endley, **Hanyang University**, Seoul, South Korea; Mauro Luiz Pinheiro, **IBEU Ceará**, Ceará, Brazil; Ana Lúcia da Costa Maia de Almeida, **IBEU Copacabana**, Copacabana, Brazil; Maristela Silva, **ICBEU Manaus**, Manaus, Brazil; Magaly Mendes Lemos, **ICBEU São José dos Campos**, São José dos Campos, Brazil; Augusto Pelligrini Filho, **ICBEU São Luis**, São Luis, Brazil; Leonardo Mercado, **ICPNA**, Lima, Peru; Lucia Rangel Lugo, **Instituto Tecnológico de San Luis Potosí**, San Luis Potosí, Mexico; Maria Guadalupe Hernández Lozada, **Instituto Tecnológico de Tlalnepantla**, Tlalnepantla de Baz, Mexico; Karen Stewart, **International House Veracruz**, Veracruz, Mexico; Tom David, **Japan College of Foreign Languages**, Tokyo, Japan; Andy Burki, **Korea University, International Foreign Language School**, Seoul, South Korea; Jinseo Noh, **Kwangwoon University**, Seoul, South Korea; Neil Donachey, **La Salle Junior and Senior High School**, Kagoshima, Japan; Rich Hollingworth, **La Salle Junior and Senior High School**, Kagoshima, Japan; Quentin Kum, **La Salle Junior and Senior High School**, Kagoshima, Japan; Geoff Oliver, **La Salle Junior and Senior High School**, Kagoshima, Japan; Martin Williams, **La Salle Junior and Senior High School**, Kagoshima, Japan; Nadezhda Nazarenko, **Lone Star College**, Houston, TX, USA; Carolyn Ho, **Lone Star College-Cy-Fair**, Cypress, TX, USA; Kaoru Kuwajima, Meijo University, Nagoya, Japan; Alice Ya-fen Chou, **National Taiwan University of Science and Technology**, Taipei, Taiwan; Raymond Dreyer, **Northern Essex Community College**, Lawrence, MA, USA; Mary Keter Terzian Megale, **One Way Línguas-Suzano**, São Paulo, Brazil; B. Greg Dunne, **Osaka Shoin Women's University**, Higashi-Osaka, Japan; Robert Maran, **Osaka Shoin Women's University**, Higashi-Osaka, Japan; Bonnie Cheeseman, **Pasadena Community College** and **UCLA American Language Center**, Los Angeles, CA, USA; Simon Banha, **Phil Young's English School**, Curitiba, Brazil; Oh Jun Il, **Pukyong National University**, Busan, South Korea; Carmen Gehrke, **Quatrum English Schools**, Porto Alegre, Brazil; John Duplice, **Rikkyo University**, Tokyo, Japan; Wilzania da Silva Nascimento, **Senac**, Manaus, Brazil; Miva Silva Kingston, **Senac**, Manaus, Brazil; Lais Lima, **Senac**, Manaus, Brazil; Yuan-hsun Chuang, **Soo Chow University**, Taipei, Taiwan; Mengjiao Wu, Shanghai Maritime University, Shanghai, China; Wen hsiang Su, **Shih Chien University Kaohsiung Campus**, Kaohsiung, Taiwan; Lynne Kim, **Sun Moon University (Institute for Language Education)**, Cheon An City, Chung Nam, South Korea; Regina Ramalho, **Talken English School**, Curitiba, Brazil; Tatiana Mendonça, **Talken English School**, Curitiba, Brazil; Ricardo Todeschini, **Talken English School**, Curitiba, Brazil; Monica Carvalho da Rocha, **Talken English School**, Joinville, Brazil; Karina Schoene, **Talken English School**, Joinville, Brazil; Diaña Peña Munoz and Zira Kuri, **The Anglo**, Mexico City, Mexico; Christopher Modell, **Tokai University**, Tokyo, Japan; Song-won Kim, **TTI (Teacher's Training Institute)**, Seoul, South Korea; Nancy Alarcón, **UNAM FES Zaragoza Language Center**, Mexico City, Mexico; Laura Emilia Fierro López, **Universidad Autónoma de Baja California**, Mexicali, Mexico; María del Rocío Domínguez Gaona, **Universidad Autónoma de Baja California**, Tijuana, Mexico; Saul Santos Garcia, **Universidad Autónoma de Nayarit**, Nayarit, Mexico;Christian Meléndez, **Universidad Católica de El Salvador**, San Salvador, El Salvador; Irasema Mora Pablo, **Universidad de Guanajuato**, Guanajuato, Mexico; Alberto Peto, **Universidad de Oaxaca**, Tehuantepec, Mexico; Carolina Rodriguez Beltan, **Universidad Manuela Beltrán, Centro Colombo Americano**, and **Universidad Jorge Tadeo Lozano**, Bogotá, Colombia; Nidia Milena Molina Rodriguez, **Universidad Manuela Beltrán** and **Universidad Militar Nueva Granada**, Bogotá, Colombia; Yolima Perez Arias, **Universidad Nacional de Colombia**, Bogotá, Colombia; Héctor Vázquez García, **Universidad Nacional Autónoma de Mexico**, Mexico City, Mexico; Pilar Barrera, **Universidad Técnica de Ambato**, Ambato, Ecuador; Doborah Hulston, **University of Regina**, Regina, Canada; Rebecca J. Shelton, **Valparaiso University, Interlink Language Center**, Valparaiso, IN, USA; Tae Lee, **Yonsei University**, Seodaemun-gu, Seoul, South Korea; Claudia Thereza Nascimento Mendes, **York Language Institute**, Rio de Janeiro, Brazil; Jamila Jenny Hakam, **ELT Consultant**, Muscat, Oman; Stephanie Smith, **ELT Consultant**, Austin, TX, USA.

Scope and sequence

LEVEL 2	Learning outcomes	Grammar	Vocabulary
Welcome Unit Pages 2–3 **Classroom language** Page 4	**Students can...** ☑ ask questions about English words		Classroom instructions
Unit 1 Pages 5–14			
My interests **A** *I'm interested in fashion.* **B** *Can you repeat that please?* **C** *Do you play sports?* **D** *Free time*	**Students can...** ☑ ask and talk about interests ☑ ask for repetition ☑ ask someone to speak more slowly ☑ ask and talk about sports and exercise habits ☑ talk about people's free-time activities	Present of *be* Simple present	Interests Sports and exercise
Unit 2 Pages 15–24			
Descriptions **A** *He's talkative and friendly.* **B** *I don't think so.* **C** *What do they look like?* **D** *People's profiles*	**Students can...** ☑ ask and talk about people's personalities ☑ say they think something is true and not true ☑ ask and talk about people's appearances ☑ describe their personality and appearance	*What . . . like?*; *be* + adjective (+ noun) *What . . . look like?*; order of adjectives	Personality adjectives Appearance
Unit 3 Pages 25–34			
Rain or shine **A** *It's extremely cold.* **B** *In my opinion, . . .* **C** *I'd like to play chess.* **D** *Where would you like to go?*	**Students can...** ☑ talk about the weather and seasons ☑ ask for and give an opinion ☑ talk about what they would like to do ☑ talk about a place they would like to visit	Adverbs of intensity; quantifiers with verbs *Would like* + infinitive	Weather Indoor activities
Unit 4 Pages 35–44			
Life at home **A** *There's a lot of light.* **B** *Can you turn down the music?* **C** *I always hang up my clothes!* **D** *What a home!*	**Students can...** ☑ ask and answer questions about their home ☑ make and agree to requests ☑ talk about household chores ☑ describe a home	*How many / much*; quantifiers before nouns Separable two-word phrasal verbs	Things in a home Household chores
Unit 5 Pages 45–54			
Health **A** *Breathe deeply.* **B** *I'm not feeling well.* **C** *How healthy are you?* **D** *Don't stress out!*	**Students can...** ☑ give and follow instructions ☑ say how they feel ☑ wish someone well ☑ ask and talk about healthy habits ☑ discuss ways to manage stress	Imperatives; adverbs of manner *How* questions	Parts of the body Healthy habits
Unit 6 Pages 55–64			
What's on TV? **A** *I love watching game shows.* **B** *I don't really agree.* **C** *I'm recording a documentary.* **D** *Popular TV*	**Students can...** ☑ talk about types of TV shows they like ☑ agree and disagree with an opinion ☑ describe future plans ☑ give their opinions about popular TV shows	Verb + infinitive or gerund Present continuous for future plans	Types of TV shows Television

Functional language	Listening and Pronunciation	Reading and Writing	Speaking
			• Discussion about English words
Interactions: Asking for repetition Asking someone to speak more slowly	**Listening:** About a party An unusual interest **Pronunciation:** Intonation in *yes* / *no* and *Wh-* questions	**Reading:** "What's your hobby?" Social media posts **Writing:** An interest	• Interview about interests • *Keep talking:* Board game about favorites • Class contact list • Interview about sports and exercise • *Keep talking:* "Find someone who" activity about free-time activities • Discussion about other people's interests
Interactions: Saying you think something is true Saying you think something isn't true	**Listening:** People's personalities An online profile **Pronunciation:** *Is he* or *Is she*	**Reading:** "Online Profiles" A webpage **Writing:** Guess who!	• Descriptions of family member personalities • *Keep talking*: Quiz about confidence • Discussion about people at a party • Guessing game about physical appearances • *Keep talking*: Different physical appearances • Personal descriptions
Interactions: Asking for an opinion Giving an opinion	**Listening:** Weather in different cities A good time to visit places **Pronunciation:** Reduction of *would you*	**Reading:** "Canada Through the Seasons" A brochure **Writing:** An email to a friend	• True or false information about the weather • *Keep talking*: Information gap activity about the weather • Opinions about the weather • Decisions about things to do • *Keep talking*: Things to do someday • Discussion about places to visit
Interactions: Making a request Agreeing to a request	**Listening:** Friendly requests A tour of Graceland **Pronunciation:** Intonation in requests	**Reading:** "Unusual Homes from Around the World" An online article **Writing:** Dream home	• Discussion about homes • *Keep talking*: Memory game about a home • Problems and requests • Interview about chores • *Keep talking*: Decisions about chores • Discussion of a dream home
Interactions: Saying how you feel Wishing someone well	**Listening:** What's wrong? Creative ways to manage stress **Pronunciation:** Reduction of *and*	**Reading:** "Feeling Stressed?" An online article **Writing:** Managing stress	• Instructions • *Keep talking*: Exercises at your desk • Role play about health problems and not feeling well • Questions about healthy habits • *Keep talking*: Quiz about health • Tips for living with stress
Interactions: Agreeing with an opinion Disagreeing with an opinion	**Listening:** What to watch on TV Favorite TV shows **Pronunciation:** Sentence stress	**Reading:** "Reality Shows" An online article **Writing:** My favorite TV show	• "Find someone who" activity about TV preferences • *Keep talking*: Debate about things to watch • Opinions about television • List of shows to record • *Keep talking*: Plans for tomorrow • Discussion about reality TV shows

LEVEL 2	Learning outcomes	Grammar	Vocabulary
Unit 7 Pages 65–74			
Shopping **A** *It's lighter and thinner.* **B** *Would you take $10?* **C** *This hat is too small.* **D** *A shopper's paradise*	**Students can...** ☑ describe and compare products ☑ bargain ☑ describe how clothing looks and fits ☑ discuss good places to shop	Comparative adjectives *Enough* and *too*	Opposites Adjectives to describe clothing
Unit 8 Pages 75–84			
Fun in the city **A** *You shouldn't miss it!* **B** *I'd recommend going . . .* **C** *The best and the worst* **D** *The best place to go*	**Students can...** ☑ say what people should do in a city ☑ ask for and give a recommendation ☑ make comparisons about their city ☑ discuss aspects of a city	*Should* for recommendations; *can* for possibility Superlative adjectives	Places to see Adjectives to describe
Unit 9 Pages 85–94			
People **A** *Where was he born?* **B** *I'm not sure, but I think . . .* **C** *People I admire* **D** *Making a difference*	**Students can...** ☑ ask and talk about people from the past ☑ express certainty and uncertainty ☑ describe people they admire ☑ describe people who made a difference	*Was / were* born; past of *be* Simple past; *ago*	Careers Personality adjectives
Unit 10 Pages 95–104			
In a restaurant **A** *The ice cream is fantastic!* **B** *I'll have the fish, please.* **C** *Have you ever . . .?* **D** *Restaurant experiences*	**Students can...** ☑ talk about menus and eating out ☑ order food in a restaurant ☑ ask about and describe food experiences ☑ describe restaurant experiences	Articles Present perfect for experience	Menu items Interesting food
Unit 11 Pages 105–114			
Entertainment **A** *I'm not a fan of dramas.* **B** *Any suggestions?* **C** *All of us love music.* **D** *Singing shows around the world*	**Students can...** ☑ talk about their movie habits and opinions ☑ ask for and give suggestions ☑ report the results of a survey ☑ describe important singers and musicians	*So, too, either,* and *neither* Determiners	Types of movies Types of music
Unit 12 Pages 115–124			
Time for a change **A** *Personal change* **B** *I'm happy to hear that!* **C** *I think I'll get a job.* **D** *Dreams and aspirations*	**Students can...** ☑ give reasons for personal changes ☑ react to good and bad news ☑ make predictions about the future ☑ discuss their dreams for the future	Infinitives of purpose *Will* for predictions; *may, might* for possibility	Personal goals Milestones

Functional language	Listening and Pronunciation	Reading and Writing	Speaking
Interactions: Bargaining for a lower price Suggesting a different price	**Listening:** Bargaining at a yard sale A weekend market in London **Pronunciation:** Linked sounds	**Reading:** "Chatucak Weekend Market" A webpage **Writing:** An interesting market	• Comparison of two products • *Keep talking*: Comparing several products • Role play of a bargaining situation • Discussion about clothes • *Keep talking*: Different clothing items • Discussion about good places to shop
Interactions: Asking for a recommendation Giving a recommendation	**Listening:** Cities At a tourist information desk **Pronunciation:** Word stress	**Reading:** "Austin or San Antonio?" A message board **Writing:** A message board	• Discussion about things to do in one day • *Keep talking*: Discussion of possible things to do • Role play at a tourist information desk • Comparison of places in a town or a city • *Keep talking*: City quiz • Discussion about aspects of a city
Interactions: Expressing certainty Expressing uncertainty	**Listening:** Friends playing a board game People who made a difference **Pronunciation:** Simple past *-ed* endings	**Reading:** "A Different Kind of Banker" A biography **Writing:** A biography	• Guessing game about famous people • *Keep talking*: Information gap activity about people from the past • Group quiz about famous people • Descriptions of admirable people • *Keep talking*: Discussion about inspiring people • Description of a person who made a difference
Interactions: Ordering food Checking information	**Listening:** Customers ordering food Restaurant impressions **Pronunciation:** *The* before vowel and consonant sounds	**Reading:** "Restaurants with a Difference" A webpage **Writing:** A review	• Discussion about eating out • *Keep talking*: A menu • Role play of a restaurant situation • Discussion about food experiences • *Keep talking*: Board game about food experiences • Restaurant recommendations
Interactions: Asking for suggestions Giving a suggestion	**Listening:** Fun things to do An influential world musician **Pronunciation:** Reduction of *of*	**Reading:** "Everybody Loves a Sing-Off" An online article **Writing:** A popular musician	• Movie talk • *Keep talking*: Movie favorites • Suggestions about the weekend • Class musical preferences • *Keep talking*: Class survey about music • A playlist
Interactions: Reacting to bad news Reacting to good news	**Listening:** Sharing news An interview with an athlete **Pronunciation:** Contraction of *will*	**Reading:** "An Olympic Dream Flies High" An online article **Writing:** A dream come true	• Discussion about changes • *Keep talking:* Reasons for doing things • Good news and bad news • Predictions about the future • *Keep talking*: Predictions about next year • Dream planner

Welcome

1 Working with a partner

A **Complete the conversations with the correct sentences. Then listen and check your answers.**

- Can I borrow your pen?
- Let's compare our answers!
- Whose turn is it?
- Are you ready?

B PAIR WORK **Practice the conversations.**

2 Asking for help

A Match the questions and answers. Then practice with a partner.

1 How do you spell this word? __d__ a You say "welcome."
2 How do you pronounce this word? _____ b It means "not common."
3 What does this word mean? _____ c /ˈhabi/ (hobby).
4 How do you say *bienvenidos* in English? _____ d I-N-T-E-R-A-C-T-I-O-N-S.

B Write these four questions in the conversations. Then compare with a partner.

What does this word mean?	How do you say *Boa sorte* in English?
How do you pronounce this word?	How do you spell your first name?

1 A ______________________________
B /ˈkɑntɛkst/ (context).
A Oh, that's easy!

2 A ______________________________
B I think it means "working together."
A Just like us!

3 A ______________________________
B E-M-I-K-O.
A That's a nice name.

4 A ______________________________
B You say "Good luck."
A I see. Well, good luck!

C Listen and check your answers. Then practice the conversations with a partner.

3 Speaking Do you know?

A PAIR WORK Think of two English words you know. Ask your partner about them.

A: *What does the word kitten mean?*
B: *It means "baby cat."*

B PAIR WORK Look at a page in the book and find two words. Write one word in each blank. Ask about the words.

How do you spell this word? ____________________ How do you pronounce this word? ____________________

C GROUP WORK Think of words or expressions that you want to know in English. Ask your group how to say them. Can they answer?

A: How do you say ________________ in English?
B: You say "________________."

I can ask questions about English words.

Classroom language

A **Write these actions below the correct picture. Then compare with a partner.**

Close your books.	Look at the picture.	Turn to page . . .
Listen.	✓Open your books.	Work in groups.
Look at the board.	Raise your hand.	Work in pairs.

1 Open your books.

2 ____________

3 ____________

4 ____________

5 ____________

6 ____________

7 ____________

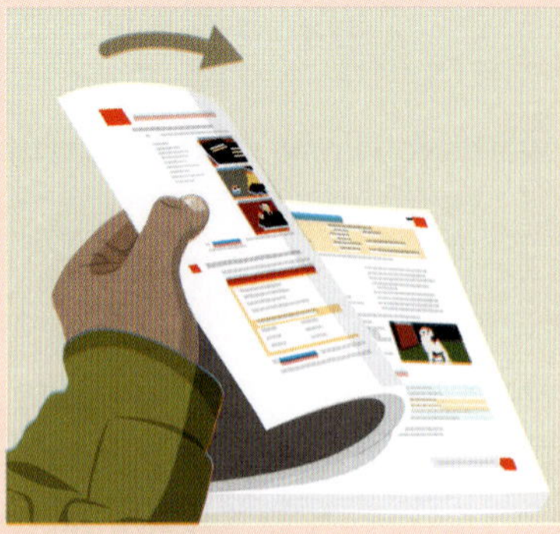

8 ____________

9 ____________

A: What's number one?

B: It's . . .

B **Listen and check your answers.**

C **Listen to seven of the actions. Do each one.**

1 My interests

Lesson A

- Interests
- Present of *be*

Lesson B

- Asking for repetition
- Asking someone to speak more slowly

Lesson C

- Sports and exercise
- Simple present

Lesson D

- Reading: "What's your hobby?"
- Writing: An interest

Warm Up

A Name the things in the pictures. What do you think each person likes? Why?

B Do you like similar things?

A I'm interested in fashion.

1 Vocabulary Interests

A Match the words and the pictures. Then listen and check your answers.

a art
b fashion
c languages
d literature
e politics
f pop culture
g sports
h technology
i travel

1 *d*

2 ___

3 ___

4 ___

5 ___

6 ___

7 ___

8 ___

9 ___

2 Language in context Find new friends!

A Read the survey. Then complete the survey with your own information.

LOOKING FOR NEW FRIENDS?
FIND SOMEONE WITH SIMILAR INTERESTS!

What's your name? ______
Where are you from? ______
How old are you? ______
Are you single or married? ______

Are you interested in . . . ?

travel	☐ yes	☐ no
sports	☐ yes	☐ no
fashion	☐ yes	☐ no

Who's your favorite . . . ?
actor ______
actress ______
singer ______

What's your favorite . . . ?
TV show ______
movie ______
video game ______

B GROUP WORK Compare your information. Who are you similar to? How?

"Ming and I are similar. Our favorite movie is . . ."

3 Grammar Present of *be*

Where **are** you from? I**'m** from South Korea. How old **is** he? He**'s** 22 years old. What **are** your friends' names? Their names **are** Ming and Kathy.	**Are** you interested in travel? Yes, I **am**. No, I**'m not**. **Is** he single? Yes, he **is**. No, he**'s not**. / No, he **isn't**. **Are** they married? Yes, they **are**. No, they**'re not**. / No, they **aren't**.

A Complete the conversations with the correct form of *be*. Then practice with a partner.

1
A What *'s* ________ your name?
B Diego.
A Where ________ you from?
B Mexico City.
A ________ you single?
B No, I ________ not. I ________ married.
A ________ you interested in fashion?
B Not really. I ________ interested in sports.

2
A Where ________ your parents from?
B My mother ________ from Osaka.
A ________ your father from Osaka, too?
B No, he ________. He ________ from Nagoya.
A What ________ they interested in?
B Art, languages, and literature.
A ________ they interested in travel?
B No, they ________.

B Read the answers. Write the possible questions. Then compare with a partner.

1 *What are you interested in?* Technology.
2 ________ I'm 20 years old.
3 ________ Taylor Swift.
4 ________ No, I'm from Seoul.
5 ________ Yes, I am.

C PAIR WORK Ask and answer the questions in Part B. Answer with your own information.

4 Speaking What are you interested in?

A PAIR WORK Interview your partner. Take notes.

1 Are you interested in literature? YES → *Who's your favorite writer?* NO → *What books are in your house?*

2 Are you interested in technology? YES → *What's a good cell phone?* NO → *How old is your cell phone?*

3 Are you and your friends interested in similar things? YES → *What are you and your friends interested in?* NO → *What are your friends interested in?*

B PAIR WORK Tell another classmate about your partner's answers.

"Elena is interested in literature. Her favorite author is Jane Austen."

5 Keep talking!

Go to page 125 for more practice.

I can ask and talk about interests.

B Can you repeat that, please?

1 Interactions Asking for repetition

A Look at the pictures. Where are the people? What do you think they're talking about?

B Listen to the conversations. Were your guesses from Part A correct? Then practice the conversations.

Fred: Fun party.
Carlos: Yeah, it is. Um, do you have the time?
Fred: It's . . . 9:50.
Carlos: I'm sorry. Can you repeat that, please?
Fred: Sure. It's 9:50.
Carlos: Wow! It's late.

Meg: So call me. OK?
Melissa: Sure. What's your number?
Meg: It's 629-555-0193.
Melissa: Can you say that more slowly, please?
Meg: Oh, sure. It's 629-555-0193.
Melissa: Got it. Thanks.

C Listen to the expressions. Then practice the conversations again with the new expressions.

Asking for repetition

- Can you repeat that, please?
- Could you repeat that, please?
- Could you say that again, please?

Asking for someone to speak more slowly

- Can you say that more slowly, please?
- Could you say that more slowly, please?
- Could you speak more slowly, please?

D Put the words in order. Then practice the questions with a partner.

1. you / can / that / please / repeat — *Can you repeat that, please?*
2. slowly / please / say / you / can / more / that — ______
3. again / could / say / you / that / please — ______
4. slowly / please / more / you / speak / could — ______

2 Pronunciation Intonation in *yes / no* and *Wh-* questions

A **Listen and repeat. Notice the intonation in *yes / no* and *Wh-* questions.**

Do you have the time? ↗ Are you interested in fashion? ↗

Where are you from? ↘ What's your number? ↘

B **Listen and mark the intonation in the questions. Then practice with a partner.**

1 Who's your favorite actress?
2 Do you like parties?
3 Are you from here?
4 What's your email address?

3 Listening Could you . . . ?

A **Listen to Clara's phone calls. Who does she talk to? Number the pictures from 1 to 3.**

B **Listen again. Check (✓) the question that Clara is going to ask at the end of each conversation.**

1 ☐ Can you repeat that, please? ☐ Can you say that more slowly, please?
2 ☐ Could you repeat that, please? ☐ Could you say that more slowly, please?
3 ☐ Could you say that again, please? ☐ Could you speak more slowly, please?

4 Speaking Class contact list

A GROUP WORK **Ask four classmates their name, email address, and birthday. Make a list. Ask them to repeat or speak more slowly if necessary.**

	Full name	Email address	Birthday
1			
2			
3			
4			

A: What's your full name?
B: It's Maria Sanchez.
A: I'm sorry. Could you . . . ?

B **Share your information and create a class contact list.**

I can ask someone to speak more slowly. ✓

C Do you play sports?

1 Vocabulary Sports and exercise

A These people are very active. Match the sentences and the pictures. Then listen and check your answers.

They . . .
- bowl. ______
- ski. ______
- swim. ______

a

b

c

They play . . .
- baseball. ______
- golf. ______
- table tennis. ______

d

e

f

They do . . .
- gymnastics. ______
- karate. ______
- yoga. ______

g

h

i

B PAIR WORK Which sports and exercises in Part A do you do? Tell your partner.

"I swim and play baseball."

2 Conversation A ski sale

A Listen and practice.

Clerk Can I help you?

Gina Yes, thank you. I want something for my boyfriend. It's his birthday tomorrow.

Clerk OK. What sports does he like? Does he play baseball?

Gina No, he doesn't.

Clerk How about table tennis? You can play together.

Gina No, we don't really like table tennis.

Clerk Well, does he ski?

Gina Yes! He skis all the time. Do you sell skis?

Clerk Yes, we do. And there's a ski sale right now.

Gina Great!

B Listen to the conversation between Gina and her boyfriend. Where are they?

3 Grammar Simple present

What sports **do** you **like**?	**Do** you **sell** skis?	
I **like** golf and karate.	Yes, I **do**.	No, I **don't**.
I **don't like** basketball.		
What sports **does** he **play**?	**Does** he **play** baseball?	
He **plays** soccer.	Yes, he **does**.	No, he **doesn't**.
He **doesn't play** baseball.	**Do** they **like** table tennis?	
Where **do** they **do** yoga?	Yes, they **do**.	No, they **don't**.
They **do** yoga at home.		
They **don't do** yoga in the park.		

A Complete the paragraph with the simple present forms of the verbs. Then compare with a partner.

Every year, over a thousand men and women ________________ (compete) in the Hawaii Ironman Triathlon. A triathlon ________________ (have) three parts, but it ________________ (not / have) three winners. The person with the best time for the three races ________________ (win). They ________________ (swim) for 3.86 km, ________________ (bike) for 180 km, and then ________________ (run) for 42.2 km. The winner ________________ (get) $100,000.

B Put the words in order. Then ask and answer the questions. Answer with your own information.

1 soccer / do / play / on the weekend / you ________________
2 family / like / does / what sports / your ________________
3 best friend / your / where / does / exercise ________________
4 bowl / friends / do / your / on the weekend ________________

4 Speaking Do you . . .?

A PAIR WORK **Complete the questions in the chart. Then interview your partner. Take notes.**

1 Do you play sports on the weekend?	YES →	*What sports do you play?*
	NO →	*What do you do on the weekend?*
2 Do you watch sports on TV?	YES →	*What sports ________________?*
	NO →	*What ________________ on TV?*
3 Do you exercise in the morning?	YES →	*What ________________?*
	NO →	*When ________________?*

B PAIR WORK **Tell another classmate about your partner's answers.**

"Ricardo plays basketball and does karate on the weekend."

5 Keep talking!

Go to page 126 for more practice.

I can ask and talk about sports and exercise habits.

D Free time

1 Reading

A Look at the pictures. What is each person's hobby? Guess.

B Read the social media posts and check your guesses.

What's your hobby?

I have a really cool telescope. I usually just look at the moon, but I sometimes look at the planets, especially Mars and Jupiter. I want to discover a star someday!

Read more . . .

Be the first to like this. Comments

Posted by **Hal** 7:12 a.m.

I make Navajo jewelry in my free time. I make rings, bracelets, and necklaces. It's just a hobby, but I really enjoy it. You can see my stuff on my website.

Read more . . .

Be the first to like this. Comments

Posted by **Vicky** 9:35 a.m.

A lot of people have a pet like a cat, a fish, or a bird. But I have an unusual pet – a llama! His name is Rex, and I take him camping with me. He always carries my things.

Read more . . .

Be the first to like this. Comments

Posted by **Rafael** 11:48 a.m

I write a blog about cupcakes! I go to bakeries in my hometown and try different kinds of cupcakes. Then I write about it. All of my friends read my blog.

Read more . . .

Be the first to like this. Comments

Posted by **Nadia** 1:07 p.m.

C Read the social media posts again. Which comment follows each post? Number the comments from 1 to 4.

1 Your stuff is great! Do you sell it?

2 So where's a good place to get one?

3 Good luck! Oh, what would you name it?

4 I love the picture. What does he eat?

D PAIR WORK Which social media post do you like best? Write a comment for one of the people. Discuss your ideas.

2 Listening Is that a fish?

A 🎧 **Listen to John tell his friend about *gyotaku*. Number the pictures from 1 to 4.**

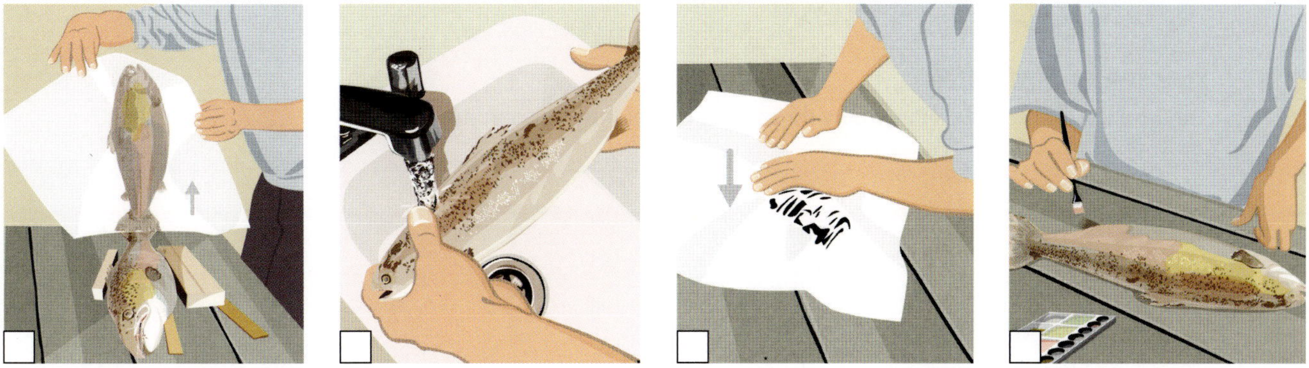

B 🎧 **Listen again. Answer the questions.**

1 Where is *gyotaku* from? ________________

2 Who does John work with? ________________

3 Is it fun? ________________

4 What does John sell? ________________

3 Writing An interest

A Think of an interest you have. Answer the questions.

- What are you interested in?
- What do you do?
- What do you like about it?

B Write a blog post about an interest you have. Use the model and your answers in Part A to help you.

Collecting Autographs

I'm interested in autographs. I collect them from baseball players. Sometimes players write their names on pieces of paper. Sometimes they write on their photos. My favorite is an autographed baseball. It's just a hobby, but I really enjoy it.

C PAIR WORK **Share your writing. Ask and answer questions for more information.**

4 Speaking Other people's interests

GROUP WORK **Think about people you know. Which of the things below do they do? Ask and answer questions for more information.**

writes a blog	wears cool clothes	has a favorite sports team
collects something	cooks a lot	makes something
travels a lot	has an unusual pet	reads a lot

A: My friend Masao writes a blog.

B: What does he write about?

A: He usually writes about sports.

C: How often do you read it?

I can *talk about people's free-time activities.* ✓

Wrap-up

1 Quick pair review

Lesson A Brainstorm!

Make a list of interests. How many do you know? You have one minute.

fashion
politics

Lesson B Do you remember?

Check (✓) the questions you can ask when someone is speaking too fast or you want someone to repeat something. You have one minute.

__✓__ Could you repeat that, please?

____ Can you say that more slowly, please?

____ What does this mean?

____ Could you say that again, please?

____ Can I speak to Rita, please?

____ Can you repeat that, please?

____ Could you speak more slowly, please?

____ How do you spell that?

Lesson C Test your partner!

Say the names of sports and exercises. Can your partner say the correct verb? You have one minute.

Student A: 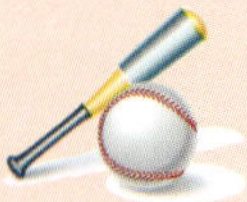  

Student B:   

A: *Baseball*

B: *Play baseball.*

Lesson D Guess!

Describe or act out an interest or a sport, but don't say its name. Can your partner guess what it is? Take turns. You and your partner have two minutes.

A: *I write online every day. Other people read my writing.*

B: *Do you write a blog?*

A: *Yes, I do.*

2 In the real world

Who has unusual interests? Go online and find someone with one of these interests. Then write about it.

has an unusual pet	collects something
makes something	plays an unusual sport

Unusual pets

A woman in the U.S. has ducks as pets . . . .

2 Descriptions

LESSON A

- Personality adjectives
- *What . . . like?*; *be* + adjective (+ noun)

LESSON B

- Saying you think something is true
- Saying you think something isn't true

LESSON C

- Appearance
- *What . . . look like?*; order of adjectives

LESSON D

- Reading: "Online Profiles"
- Writing: Guess who!

1

2

3

4

Warm Up

A Match the comments and the people in the pictures.

_______ "We love your new car!"

_______ "What a great place!"

_______ "That's very good. Good job!"

_______ "I wonder what's going to happen next."

B What else can you say about the people in the pictures?

A He's talkative and friendly.

1 Vocabulary Personality adjectives

A Match the words and pictures. Then listen and check your answers.

- a confident
- b creative
- c friendly
- d funny
- e generous
- f hardworking
- g serious
- h shy
- i talkative

1 g

2

3

4

5

6

7

8

9

B PAIR WORK **Which words describe you? Tell your partner.**

"I'm hardworking and creative. Sometimes I'm shy."

2 Language in context Find an e-pal!

A Read Nick's answers to an online form. Then complete the form with your own information.

Name	Nick Douglas
Hometown	Dallas, Texas
Age	18
What are your interests?	Fashion, literature, politics, movies, and sports
What are you like?	I'm talkative, friendly, and funny.

Name	
Hometown	
Age	
What are your interests?	
What are you like?	

B Is Nick a good e-pal for you? Why or why not?

3 Grammar *What . . . like?; be* + adjective (+ noun)

What are you like?	What's she like?	What are they like?
I'm talkative and friendly.	She's shy but friendly.	They're hardworking.
I'm **a** friendly and talkative **person**.	She's **a** shy but friendly **girl**.	They're hardworking **students**.

A Put the words in order. Then compare sentences with a partner.

1 teacher / a / Mrs. Jenkins / creative / is ______
2 Melissa / student / serious / a / is ______
3 funny / Bruno / is / talkative / and ______
4 are / Rodrigo and Miguel / confident / men ______
5 women / Marina and Elisa / are / hardworking ______
6 is / and / generous / Carrie / friendly ______

B Read the answers. Write the *What . . . like?* questions. Then practice with a partner.

1 *What are you like?* I'm serious but friendly.
2 ______ Eva is a very funny girl.
3 ______ Matt and I are talkative people.
4 ______ Mr. and Mrs. Park are generous.
5 ______ I'm very serious and hardworking.
6 ______ His brother Sam is a creative guy.

4 Speaking He's hardworking.

A PAIR WORK **Choose three people from your family. Describe them to your partner.**

brother	father	grandfather	husband
sister	mother	grandmother	wife

A: My brother's name is Gi-woo.
B: What's he like?
C: Well, he's very hardworking. He's 26 and he's an accountant. He works late every day.

B GROUP WORK **Are the people you know similar or different?**

A: My brother is really hardworking.
B: Really? My mother is hardworking, too. She's a . . .

5 Keep talking!

Go to page 127 for more practice.

I can ask and talk about people's personalities.

B I don't think so.

1 Interactions When you're not sure

A Look at the picture. Where are the people?

B Listen to the conversation. Do Will and Joe know Mike well? Then practice the conversation.

Will What's your new roommate like?
Joe Mike? Oh, he's nice, but he's not very talkative.
Will Really? Is he shy?
Joe I think so.
Will Does he know many people here?
Joe I don't think so.
Will Well, maybe we can all go out together sometime.
Joe That's a great idea.

C Listen to the expressions. Then practice the conversation again with the new expressions.

Saying you think something is true

I think so. | I believe so. | I guess so.

Saying you think something isn't true

I don't think so. | I don't believe so. | I'm not really sure.

D Complete each response with one of the expressions from Part C. Then practice with a partner.

1 A Is Rafael hardworking? B ______________ He studies a lot.
2 A Is Marilyn married? B ______________ She doesn't have a ring.
3 A Is David creative? B ______________ He paints a lot.
4 A Is Maria interested in travel? B ______________ She doesn't have a passport.
5 A Is Sun-hee friendly? B ______________ People like her.

2 Pronunciation *Is he or Is she*

A Listen and repeat. Notice the pronunciation of *Is he* and *Is she*.

/IZi/ /Iʃi/

Is he hardworking? **Is she** a good student?

B Listen and write *he* or *she*. Then practice with a partner.

1 Is ________ a creative person?
2 Is ________ your new roommate?
3 Is ________ a serious student?
4 Is ________ generous?

3 Listening People we know

A Listen to two friends talk about different people. Who are they talking about? Check (✓) the correct answers.

1 ☐ a teacher ☐ a student ☐ a friend
2 ☐ a classmate ☐ a father ☐ a neighbor
3 ☐ best friends ☐ classmates ☐ teachers

B Listen again. Circle the words you hear.

1 generous, great, funny, creative
2 talkative, hardworking, shy, friendly
3 serious, confident, nice, talkative

4 Speaking Is he friendly?

A PAIR WORK Talk about the people at the party. Use the words in the box and your own ideas.

friendly
talkative
shy
creative
serious
funny
single
married
a student
a teenager
a parent

A: Is Jun friendly?
B: I believe so
A: Is he married?
B: I don't think so.

B PAIR WORK You want to meet one person at the party. Who do you talk to? Why?

I can say I think something is true and not true.

C What do they look like?

1 Vocabulary Appearance

A Complete the descriptions with the correct words. Then listen and check your answers.

bald	middle-aged	mustache	red	short	tall

1 They're **young**. Rob is **short** and **overweight**, and May is ____________ and **thin**. Rob has **straight brown hair**. May has **blond** hair. It's ____________ and **wavy**.

2 They're ____________. Lou and Jill have **curly** ____________ hair. Jill has **shoulder-length hair**. Lou has **little round glasses**.

3 They're **elderly**. They're **medium height**. Tony is ____________ and has **a short white beard** and a ____________. Angela has **long gray** hair.

B PAIR WORK **Describe people in your family using the words in Part A.**

"My brother is young. He's ten. My father has a mustache. And my . . ."

2 Conversation That's not my husband!

A Listen and practice.

Waiter Good evening. Can I help you?

Mrs. Gray Yes, thank you. Is Ken Gray here? He's my husband.

Waiter Mr. Gray? I don't know. What does he look like?

Mrs. Gray He's tall, thin, and has black hair. And he has glasses.

Waiter Does he have a mustache?

Mrs. Gray Yes, he does.

Waiter I think he's over there.

Mrs. Gray No, that's not my husband! My husband has short hair.

B Listen to the rest of the conversation. Who is Mr. Gray with?

3 Grammar What . . . look like?; order of adjectives

What do you look like?	What does he look like?	What do they look like?
I'm short and overweight.	He's tall and thin.	They're middle-aged.
I have glasses.	He has a mustache.	They have curly red hair.

The order of adjectives is usually size, age, shape, and color.

She has **long gray** hair. (size + color) He has **little round** glasses. (size + shape)

She has **new green** glasses. (age + color) They have **curly red** hair. (shape + color)

A Look at the picture. Complete the sentences with two adjectives. Then compare with a partner.

big	brown	long	round	short	thin	wavy	young

1 He is a ________ and ________ man.
2 He has ________ hair.
3 He has a ________ beard.
4 He has ________ glasses.

B Put the words in order. Then ask and answer the questions. Answer with your own information.

1 like / what / do / look / you ________
2 best friend / look / what / does / your / like ________
3 what / like / look / does / favorite singer / your ________

4 Speaking Who is it?

PAIR WORK Describe a person in one of the pictures below, but don't say his or her name! Your partner guesses the person. Take turns.

"This person is tall and has short black hair."

5 Keep talking!

Student A go to page 128 and Student B go to page 130 for more practice.

I can ask and talk about people's appearances.

D People's profiles

1 Reading

A Read the webpage profiles. What is each person like?

Online profiles

Name: Adriano **Home:** Belo Horizonte, Brazil
Appearance: I'm tall and have long brown hair. I wear only black.
Personality: I'm a very creative person. I like to make different things from paper. I do it just for fun. I can make airplanes, birds, boats, and flowers.

Name: Bea **Home:** London, U.K.
Appearance: I'm 60, with red hair. I always wear green glasses.
Personality: I think I'm a very generous person. I have a lot of free time, so I do a lot of volunteer work at local schools. To me, it's very important to give back to my community.

Name: Suchin **Home:** Bangkok, Thailand
Appearance: I'm 30. I'm medium height and I have short hair.
Personality: I'm friendly and hardworking. I work as a salesclerk in a clothing store. We sell clothing from northern Thailand there. In my free time, I play the *seung*, a traditional musical instrument.

Name: Marco **Home:** Iquitos, Peru
Appearance: I'm tall and handsome, with long black hair.
Personality: I'm talkative and friendly. I have a part-time job. Iquitos is in the Amazon, so piranha fishing is very popular. I take tourists fishing, but we never keep the fish.

B Read the webpage again. Adriano, Bea, Suchin, and Marco later uploaded these photos to their profiles. Write the name of the person under the correct photo.

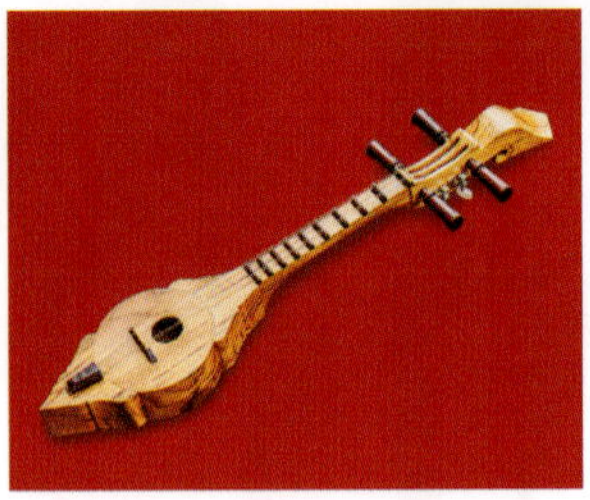

__________ __________ __________ __________

C Who wrote each sentence? Write the names.

1 ________________ But there's one problem – I can't swim!

2 ________________ My neighbors complain about the noise.

3 ________________ I especially like to work with children.

4 ________________ I spend a lot of money on paper!

D PAIR WORK Which person do you think is interesting? Why? Tell you partner.

2 Listening Starting a profile

A Listen to Brian help his mother join a social networking site. Check (✓) the picture that Linda posts on the site.

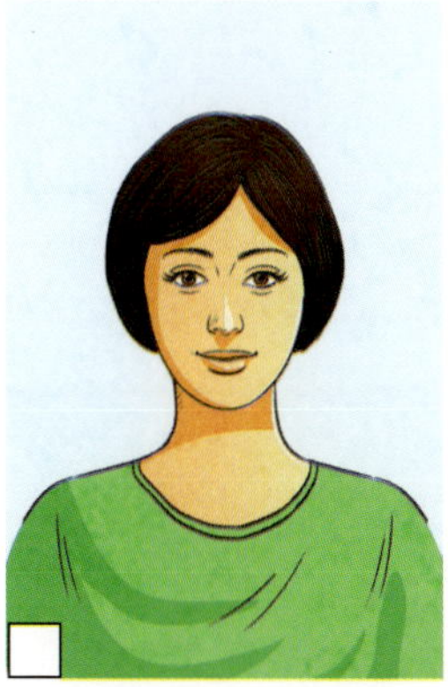

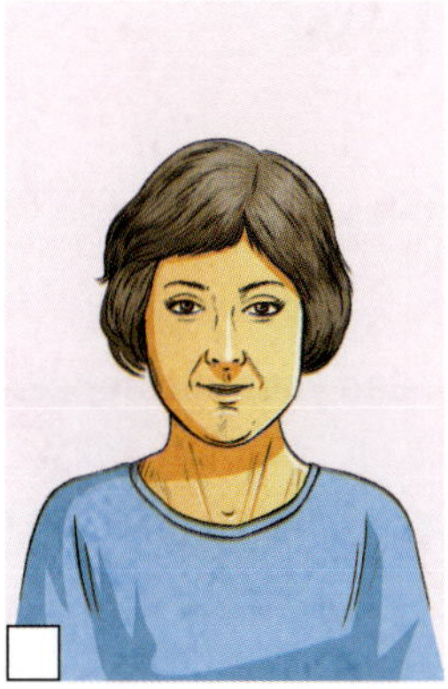

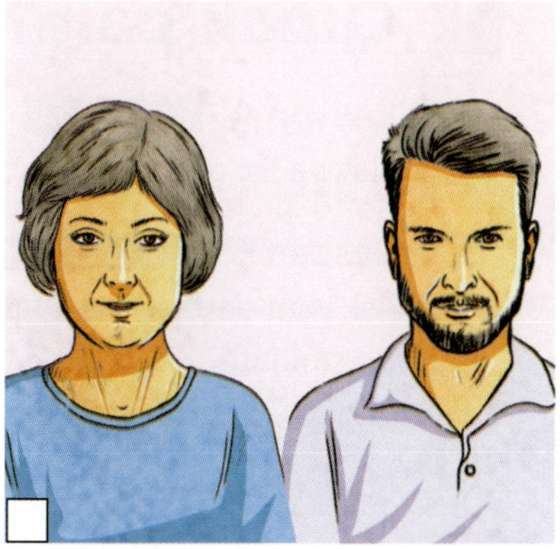

B Listen again. Check (✓) the information Brian's mother includes in her profile.

- ☐ Age
- ☐ Appearance
- ☐ Favorite actress
- ☐ Favorite singer
- ☐ Personality

3 Writing and speaking Guess who!

A Think about your appearance and personality. Answer the questions.

- How old are you?
- What do you look like?
- What are you like?

B Write a description of yourself, but don't write your name! Use the model and your answers in Part A to help you.

Guess who

I'm 18 years old. I'm thin and medium height. I have short black hair and glasses. I'm a friendly and talkative person, but sometimes I'm shy. I'm creative and very interested in art and fashion.

C GROUP WORK **Put your papers face down on the table. Take one paper and read the description. Your group guesses who it is. Take turns.**

A: This person is interested in art and fashion.

B: I think I know. Is it Marta?

A: No, Marta has long hair.
This person has short hair.

B: Oh, OK.

C: Is it . . .?

I can describe my personality and appearance. ✓

Wrap-up

1 Quick pair review

Lesson A Brainstorm!

Make a list of personality adjectives. How many do you know? You have two minutes.

Lesson B Test your partner!

Ask your partner the questions. Can your partner give the correct answers? You have one minute.

Student A: What are three ways to say you think something is true?

Student B: What are three ways to say you think something isn't true?

Lesson C Do you remember?

Look at the picture. Circle the correct word for each sentence. You have one minute.

1 This is Eduardo. He's **young** / **elderly**.
2 He has **short** / **long** gray hair.
3 His hair is **straight** / **curly**.
4 He has **little** / **big** glasses.
5 He has a **mustache** / **beard**.

Lesson D Find out!

Are any of your and your partner's friends similar? Take turns. You and your partner have two minutes.

A: My friend is tall and has long black hair. She's very funny.

B: My friend is tall and has long black hair. She's funny, too.

2 In the real world

Who are you like? Go online and find a musician, an actor, or an actress who is similar to you. Then write a description of him or her.

- What does he or she look like?
- What is he or she like?

Scarlett Johansson

Scarlett Johansson is similar to me. She's medium height. She has blond hair . . .

3 Rain or shine

Lesson A
- Weather
- Adverbs of intensity; quantifiers with verbs

Lesson B
- Asking for an opinion
- Giving an opinion

Lesson C
- Indoor activities
- *Would like* + infinitive

Lesson D
- Reading: "Canada Through the Seasons"
- Writing: An e-mail to a friend

1

2

3

4

Warm-up

A Describe the pictures. Where are the people? What are they doing?

B Do you ever do these activities? When do you do them?

A It's extremely cold.

1 Vocabulary Weather

A Label the pictures with the correct words. Then listen and check your answers.

Weather				
cloudy	rainy	snowy	sunny	windy

Temperature			
cold	cool	hot	warm

1 ______

2 ______

3 ______

4 ______

5 ______

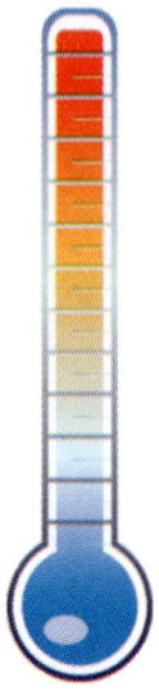

6 ______

7 ______

8 ______

9 ______

B PAIR WORK What's the weather like in your country in each season? Complete the chart with the words from Part A. Then compare answers.

spring	summer	fall	winter

rainy season	dry season

2 Language in context Favorite seasons

A Listen to people talk about their favorite season. Which places are cool?

My favorite season is spring. It's fairly cool, and rains quite a bit, but it's a good time to see the flowers.

–Jan, Lisse, Holland

I like summer a lot. It's very windy – great for windsurfing! And it doesn't rain at all.

– Fouad, Essaouira, Morocco

Fall is my favorite. It's sunny and cool, and in late October, 150 million butterflies arrive!

– Juan, Morelia, Mexico

I love winter. It's extremely cold, and it snows a lot, but that's when the Sapporo Snow Festival is.

– Rie, Sapporo, Japan

B What about you? What's your favorite season? What's the weather like then?

3 Grammar Adverbs of intensity; quantifiers with verbs

Adverbs of intensity	Quantifiers with verbs
It's **extremely** cold.	It snows **a lot**.
It's **very** windy.	It rains **quite a bit**.
It's **really** hot.	It snows **a little**.
It's **pretty** sunny.	It does**n't** rain **very much**.
It's **fairly** cool.	It does**n't** rain **at all**.
It's **somewhat** cloudy.	

Add the adverbs and quantifiers to the sentences. Then compare with a partner.

1 It snows in Moscow in the winter. (a lot) *It snows a lot in Moscow in the winter.*
2 It rains in Seattle in the winter. (quite a bit) ______
3 It's cold in Busan in January. (extremely) ______
4 It's cool in Rabat in the rainy season. (fairly) ______
5 It snows in Lima in July. (not . . . at all) ______
6 It's windy in Wellington all year. (pretty) ______

4 Listening Think about the weather!

A **Listen to people talk about the weather in three cities. Which city is one of the people planning to visit? Circle the city.**

1 Istanbul, Turkey It's ______ cold in the winter.
2 Antigua, Guatemala The ______ season is from November to April.
3 Beijing, China It's ______ and ______ in the spring.

B **Listen again. Complete the sentences with the correct words.**

5 Speaking True or false?

A **Write two true sentences and two false sentences about the weather where you live. Use these words and expressions.**

pretty sunny	rain a lot	somewhat cloudy
extremely hot	very windy	fairly cool
really cold	snow	

B PAIR WORK **Read your sentences. Your partner corrects the false sentences. Take turns.**

A: *It's pretty sunny in the winter.*
B: *I think that's false. It's somewhat cloudy in the winter.*

6 Keep talking!

Student A go to page 129 and Student B go to page 131 for more practice.

I can talk about the weather and seasons.

B In my opinion, . . .

1 Interactions Opinions

A Do you ever videochat? What do you like about it? What don't you like?

B Listen to the conversation. Where are the three people? Then practice the conversation.

Cindy So, Luk, how are things in Bangkok?

Luk Great. It's warm and sunny today.

Brian It's really cold here in Chicago. So when are you coming to see us?

Luk Well, when is a good time to visit?

Cindy Hmm . . . I'm not sure.

Luk Brian? What do you think?

Brian I think fall is a good time. The weather is great, and there's a lot to do.

Cindy Yeah, we can all go to a baseball game then.

Luk That would be great!

C Listen to the expressions. Then practice the conversation with the new expressions.

Asking for an opinion

What do you think? | What are your thoughts? | What's your opinion?

Giving an opinion

I think . . . | I'd say . . . | In my opinion, . . .

D Number the sentences from 1 to 6. Then compare with a partner.

_____ A Well . . . what's your favorite season?
__1__ A When are you going to New York?
_____ A I think spring is a great time to visit. It's usually warm and sunny then.
_____ B I don't know. What do you think? When's a good time to visit?
_____ B Really? OK. Maybe we'll go to New York in May.
_____ B My favorite season is spring.

2 Listening When's a good time to visit?

A Listen to three people talk to friends about the best time to visit these cities. Are their friends' opinions the same or different? Circle your answers.

Rio de Janeiro, Brazil

1 the same / different

Queenstown, New Zealand

2 the same / different

Marseille, France

3 the same / different

B Listen again. Write T (true) or F (false) next to the sentences.

1 Gabriel is from Rio de Janeiro, but Bianca isn't. F
2 It's very hot in Rio de Janeiro in February. ______
3 Patricia thinks it's fine to visit New Zealand anytime. ______
4 It's extremely cold in New Zealand in July and August. ______
5 Sophie is from Marseille. ______
6 A lot of stores and restaurants in France close in August. ______

3 Speaking Good time, bad time

A PAIR WORK **Discuss the weather and seasons where you live. Give your opinions.**

- When's a good season to visit?
- What months are especially good?
- What's the weather like then?
- What kinds of things do people do then?
- When's not a good time to visit? Why not?

A: *I think spring is a good time to visit Mexico. What do you think?*

B: *Yes, I'd say May is good.*

A: *The weather is warm then.*

B: *And there are some great festivals.*

B GROUP WORK **Share your opinions with another pair. Do you have the same opinions?**

I can ask for and give an opinion.

C I'd like to play chess.

1 Vocabulary Indoor activities

A Complete the phrases with the correct words. Then listen and check your answers.

a board game	cookies	a jigsaw puzzle	popcorn
chess	a crossword	a nap	a video

a bake ______

b do ______

c do ______

d make ______

e make ______

f play ______

g play ______

h take ______

B PAIR WORK **Rank these activities from 1 (fun) to 8 (not fun at all). Then compare answers.**

A: *I do a crossword every day, so I think that's really fun. How about you?*

B: *I never take a nap. I don't think that's fun at all. It's my number eight.*

2 Conversation It's raining!

A Listen and practice.

Joanie Oh, no! It's raining!

Evan We can't go on our picnic.

Joanie No. So, what would you like to do? Would you like to do a jigsaw puzzle?

Evan Not really. Would you like to play chess?

Joanie Um, yeah, I would.

Evan We can make some popcorn, too.

Joanie Great idea. But let's play a little later.

Evan OK. Why?

Joanie I'd like to take a short nap.

B Listen to their conversation later in the day. What does Evan want to do?

3 Grammar Would like + infinitive

What **would** you **like to do**?	**Would** you **like to do** a jigsaw puzzle?
I'**d like to play** chess.	Yes, I **would**. No, I **wouldn't**.
Where **would** he **like to play** chess?	Would they **like to take** a nap?
He'**d like to play** right here.	Yes, they **would**. No, they **wouldn't**.

A Circle the correct words. Then practice with a partner.

1 A Which game would you like **play** / **to play**?
  B **I'd like to** / **I would to** play chess.
2 A Would you like **do** / **to do** a crossword now?
  B No, **I'd not** / **I wouldn't**. I don't like crosswords.
3 A What **do** / **would** you like to do tonight?
  B **I'd like** / I **would** to watch TV with my friends.

B PAIR WORK **Make true sentences with *I'd like to* or *I wouldn't like to*. Tell your partner.**

have class outside	play chess after class	stay in this weekend	take a nap right now

4 Pronunciation Reduction of *would you*

A Listen and repeat. Notice how *would you* is pronounced /wʊdʒə/.

Would you like to play a board game? Which game **would you** like to play?

B PAIR WORK **Practice the questions in Exercise 3A again. Reduce *would you* to /wʊdʒə/.**

5 Speaking I'd like to . . .

A PAIR WORK **Look out these windows and describe the weather. Then decide what you'd like to do together on each day. Take notes.**

1

2

3

A: *It's cool and rainy today. What would you like to do?*
B: *I'd like to do a jigsaw puzzle. How about you?*

B GROUP WORK **Share your ideas with another pair. Ask and answer questions for more information.**

6 Keep talking!

Go to page 132 for more practice.

I can talk about what I would like to do.

D Where would you like to go?

1 Reading

A Read the article. Where do you think it is from? Check (✓) the correct answer.

☐ a vacation blog ☐ a tourist brochure ☐ a textbook ☐ a weather report

Canada Through the Seasons

The weather is very different in this large country, so there's something to do for everyone in every season.

SPRING can arrive in February in Victoria on the west coast. In other parts of Canada, it gets warm in early April, and spring weather continues until June. In British Columbia, you can kayak, camp, or take a train trip through the Rocky Mountains.

SUMMER brings warm to hot weather from May to September. This is a great time to fish in one of Canada's many lakes; kayak among the whales in Churchill, Manitoba; or have some Wild West fun at the Calgary Stampede.

FALL brings cool temperatures in September and October. It's a good time of year to see the fall leaves in eastern Canada, enjoy hiking, visit museums, or go to the Toronto International Film Festival.

Snow begins to fall in November, and temperatures drop.Days are short in **WINTER**, but you can ski, go to an ice festival, or see the northern lights. In parts of British Columbia, the snow doesn't stay long and you can golf all year!

B Read the article again. When can you use these things? Write the season.

____

____

____

____

C GROUP WORK Imagine you can visit Canada. When and where would you go? Why? Discuss your ideas.

2 Writing An email to a friend

A Think of a place and a friend you would like to visit. Answer the questions.

- What is your friend's name?
- Where does your friend live?
- When do you plan to visit?
- What would you like to do there?

B Write an email to a friend about your travel plans. Use the model and your answers in Part A to help you.

Reply Forward

From: Kate Spencer
To: Hee-jin Choi

Hi, Hee-jin,

I have good news. I can visit you in Seoul this summer! Tell me about Seoul. What's the weather like in the summer? Is it really hot?

As you know, I'm very interested in art and food. So I'd like to visit the National Museum and go to some really good restaurants. What about you? What would you like to do?

This is so exciting! See you soon.

Kate

C PAIR WORK **Share your writing. Ask and answer questions for more information.**

3 Speaking A place I'd like to visit

A Think about a place you'd like to visit in your own country or a different country. Take notes.

Place: ________ When would you like to go?	Why would you like to go then?	What would you like to do there?

B GROUP WORK **Share your ideas. Ask and answer questions for more information.**

A: I'd really like to go to Kyoto in the spring.
B: Why would you like to go then?
A: Because I'd like to see the cherry blossoms.
C: What else would you like to do there?

I can talk about a place I'd like to visit.

Wrap-up

1 Quick pair review

Lesson A Brainstorm!

Make a list of words for weather and words for temperature. How many do you know? You have two minutes.

Lesson B Do you remember?

Check (✓) the questions you can ask when you want someone's opinion. You have one minute.

- ☐ What's your opinion?
- ☐ What's your teacher's name?
- ☐ What's the weather like today?
- ☐ What are your thoughts?
- ☐ What are you like?
- ☐ What do you think?

Lesson C Find out!

What is one thing both you and your partner would like to do outside this weekend? What is one thing you both would like to do inside? Take turns. You and your partner have two minutes.

A: *I'd like to play chess inside. Would you?*

B: *No. I'd like to bake cookies. Would you?*

A: *Yes, I would.*

Lesson D Guess!

Describe a famous place in your country, but don't say its name. Can your partner guess where it is? Take turns. You and your partner have two minutes.

A: *It's hot, and it's a big city. People have parties on the beach.*

B: *Is it Rio de Janeiro?*

A: *Yes, it is.*

2 In the real world

Where would you like to go? Go online and find the typical weather for that place in every season. Then write about it.

Chicago

I'd like to go to Chicago. There are four seasons. It's extremely cold in the winter. It's very windy in the spring . . .

4 Life at home

LESSON A
- Things in a home
- *How many/much;* quantifiers before nouns

LESSON B
- Making a request
- Agreeing to a request

LESSON C
- Household chores
- Separable two-word phrasal verbs

LESSON D
- Reading: Unusual Homes from around the World
- Writing: Dream home

A 

B 

C 

D 

Warm Up

A These are the homes of world leaders. Match the countries and the pictures. Check your answers on page 44.

_____ Brazil _____ France _____ Iceland _____ Japan

B Rank the homes you would like to visit from 1 (really want to visit) to 4 (don't want to visit).

A There's a lot of light.

1 Vocabulary Things in a home

A Label the pictures with the correct words. Then listen and check your answers.

bathtub	bed	coffee table	refrigerator

B PAIR WORK **Which of the things in Part A do you have in your home? Tell your partner.**

2 Language in context A new apartment

A Listen to the conversation. Beth has a new apartment. Which room does Lori like?

Lori Your new place is nice. How many rooms are there?

Beth There are four – a kitchen, a living room, a bathroom, and a bedroom.

Lori I really like your kitchen.

Beth Thanks. There aren't many cupboards, and there isn't much space, but that's OK. I hardly ever cook.

Lori Look at all the windows in your living room!

Beth Yeah, there's a lot of light in here. But . . . there's also a lot of noise!

B **What about you? What is important to you when you move into a new house or apartment?**

3 Grammar *How many/much;* quantifiers before nouns

How many cupboards are there?		
	a lot of	
There are	**some**	cupboards.
	a few	
There **aren't**	**many**	cupboards.
	any	

How much light is there?		
	a lot of	
There's	**some**	light.
	a little	
There **isn't**	**much**	light.
	any	

A **Complete the questions with *many* or *much*. Answer the questions about the home in Exercise 1. Then practice with a partner.**

1 How ________ space is there in the kitchen? ________

2 Are there ________ cupboards in the kitchen? ________

3 How ________ chairs are there in the living room? ________

4 Are there ________ shelves in the bathroom? ________

5 How ________ light is there in the bedroom? ________

B PAIR WORK **Ask and answer questions about the apartment in Exercise 2.**

rooms / apartment	cupboards / kitchen	space / kitchen
light / living room	windows / living room	noise / apartment

A: *How many rooms are there in the apartment?*

B: *There are four rooms. Are there many cupboards in the kitchen?*

4 Speaking My home

PAIR WORK **Add three questions below. Then interview your partner. Find out three things that are similar about your homes.**

- Do you live in a house or apartment?
- How many rooms are there?
- Are there many closets in the bedroom?
- Is there much space in the bathroom?

____

____

____

A: *Do you live in a house or apartment?*

B: *I live in a small apartment.*

A: *Me, too.*

house

apartment

5 Keep talking!

Go to page 133 for more practice.

I can ask and answer questions about my home.

B Can you turn down the music?

1 Interactions Requests

A What are your neighbors like? Do you like them?

B Listen to the conversation. Why does Keisha call her neighbor? Then practice the conversation.

Carlos Hello?

Keisha Hi. It's Keisha from downstairs. Are you having a party?

Carlos Uh-huh. Are we being noisy?

Keisha I'm afraid so. Can you turn down the music, please?

Carlos Sure. I can do it now.

Keisha Thank you. I have an exam tomorrow, and I'm trying to study.

Carlos I understand.

Keisha Thanks again.

C Listen to the expressions. Then practice the conversation again with the new expressions.

Making a request	Agreeing to a request
Can you turn down the music, please?	Sure.
Could you turn down the music, please?	No problem.
Would you turn down the music, please?	I'd be happy to.

D Match the requests and the responses. Then practice with a partner.

1 Can you turn down your TV, please?
2 Can you move your car, please?
3 Could you answer the phone, please?
4 Would you open the curtains, please?

a I'd be happy to. I'm going to work now, anyway.
b Sure. I think it's for me.
c No problem. Sorry about the noise.
d Sure. There isn't much light in here.

2 Pronunciation Intonation in requests

A **Listen and repeat. Notice the falling intonation in these requests.**

Can you turn down the music, please? ↘ Can you move your car, please? ↘

B **PAIR WORK Practice the questions in Exercise 1D again. Pay attention to your intonation.**

3 Listening Friendly requests

A **Listen to three people call their neighbors. Where does each caller live? Circle the correct answers.**

1 apartment / house 2 apartment / house 3 apartment / house

B **Listen again. What does each caller want the neighbor to do? Check (✓) the correct answers.**

1	2	3
☐ stop the party	☐ get the cat	☐ stop exercising
☐ turn down the TV	☐ move the car	☐ exercise earlier
☐ turn down the music	☐ buy some milk	☐ stop the party

4 Speaking Neighbor to neighbor

A **Match the requests and the problems.**

1 Can you move it, please?
2 Could you put it in the garbage can, please?
3 Could you come and get it, please?
4 Would you keep it down, please?

☐ Your neighbor's cat is at your door.

☐ Your neighbor's guests are very noisy.

☐ Your neighbor's car is in your parking space.

☐ Your neighbor's garbage isn't in the garbage can.

B **PAIR WORK Call your neighbor. Identify yourself and explain the situation. Make a request. Take turns.**

A: *Hello.*
B: *Hi. It's Mike from downstairs. Your cat is at my door. Could you come and get it, please?*
A: *Sure. I'd be happy to.*

C **PAIR WORK Think of two more requests. Then call your partner to make the requests. Take turns.**

I can make and agree to requests. ✓

C I always hang up my clothes!

1 Vocabulary Household chores

A **Label the pictures with the correct words. Then listen and check your answers.**

clean out the closet	drop off the dry cleaning	pick up the magazines	take out the garbage
clean up the yard	hang up the clothes	put away the dishes	wipe off the counter

1 ______________

2 ______________

3 ______________

4 ______________

5 ______________

6 ______________

7 ______________

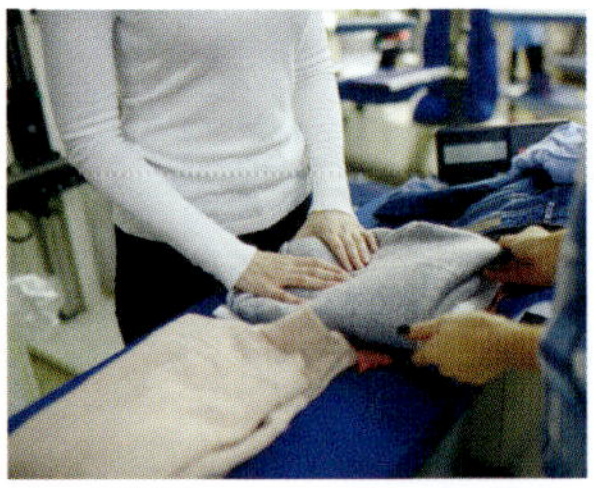

8 ______________

B PAIR WORK **Which chores in Part A do you do? Tell your partner.**

"I always clean up the yard on the weekend. I also drop off the dry cleaning."

2 Conversation Let's clean it up!

A **Listen and practice.**

Ken This place is a mess. Let's clean it up before Mom and Dad get home.

Paul Good idea. Well, I can put the dishes away and wipe off the counter.

Ken And, the garbage is full. Could you take it out?

Paul Sure. No problem.

Ken And you know, your bedroom is a mess, too. Your clothes are all over the floor. Would you pick them up, please?

Paul Yeah, I guess.

Ken And then hang them up in the closet?

Paul OK, but what are *you* going to do?

B **Listen to the rest of the conversation. What chore is Ken going to do?**

3 Grammar Separable two-word phrasal verbs

I **take out** the garbage.	Could you **hang up** your clothes, please?
I **take** the garbage **out**.	Could you **hang** your clothes **up**, please?
I **take** it **out**.	Could you **hang** them **up**, please?
Not: ~~I take out it.~~	*Not:* ~~Could you hang up them, please?~~

A Rewrite the sentences. Then compare with a partner.

1 Let's hang up the dry cleaning. *Let's hang the dry cleaning up.*
2 Could you put away your clothes, please? ____________
3 How often do you take out the garbage? ____________
4 I clean out my closets once a year. ____________

B Complete the sentences with the correct verbs. Use either *it* or *them*. Then compare with a partner.

clean out	drop off	pick up	take out
✓ clean up	hang up	put away	wipe off

1 The living room is a mess. Let's *clean it up* before the party.
2 Why is your coat on the chair? Can you ____________ in the closet?
3 The garbage is full. Could you ____________ right away, please?
4 This closet is full of old clothes and books. Let's ____________.
5 The dishes are in the dishwasher. Would you ____________ for me?
6 This table isn't clean. Can you ____________ before dinner, please?
7 These books belong to the library. Could you ____________ for me?
8 Your magazines are all over the floor. Would you ____________, please?

4 Speaking What a chore!

A PAIR WORK Interview your partner. Check (✓) his or her answers.

How often do you . . .?	My partner	How often do you . . .?	My partner
1 put away the dishes		4 clean out your closet	
2 clean up your bedroom		5 hang up your clothes	
3 take out the garbage			

B GROUP WORK Tell your group about your partner's answers. Who does a lot of chores? Who doesn't?

"Daniel does a lot of chores. He puts away the dishes and takes out the garbage every day."

5 Keep talking!

Go to page 134 for more practice.

I can talk about household chores. ✓

D What a home!

1 Reading

A Look at the pictures. Describe each home.

B Read the article. Check (✓) the best title for the article.

- [ ] Crazy Houses in the United States
- [ ] Daily Life in a Strange House
- [ ] Unusual Homes from Around the World
- [ ] How to Build Your Dream Home

The Storybook House

The classic children's story "Hansel and Gretel" inspired this unusual home in the U.S. The owners built the house by hand and included five fireplaces inside.

The Shoe House

This house in the U.S. has a living room, two bathrooms, a kitchen, and three bedrooms. There's even a shoe mailbox. The owner had a few shoe stores. No one lives there now, but there are tours of the house.

The Crazy House

People in Vietnam call this house the Crazy House because it looks strange. Part of the house is a tree, and it has unusual twists and turns. You can also see big animals on the outside. The house is a hotel and a tourist attraction.

The Upside-down House

In this house in Poland, the furniture hangs from the ceiling! No one lives there, but it's a popular tourist attraction. It took the workers a long time to build the house. They often felt sick inside.

C Read the article again. Answer the questions.

1. How did the owners build the Storybook House? ____________
2. How many rooms are there in the Shoe House? ____________
3. What can you see on the outside of the Crazy House? ____________
4. What is unusual about the inside of the Upside-down House? ____________

D PAIR WORK Which house would you like to stay in? Why? Tell your partner.

2 Listening A tour of Graceland

A **Graceland was Elvis Presley's home in Memphis, Tennessee. Look at the pictures in Part B of four rooms in the home. What do you see? What do you think the house is like?**

B **Listen to Sam and Haley take a tour of Graceland. Number the rooms from 1 to 4.**

☐ TV room

☐ kitchen

☐ dining room

☐ living room

C **Listen again. What is each person's favorite room? Complete the sentences.**

1 Sam's favorite room is the ______________________.

2 Haley's favorite room is the ______________________.

3 Writing and speaking Dream Home

A **Imagine your dream home. Answer the questions.**

- Where is your dream home?
- How many rooms does it have?
- What does it look like?
- Is there anything unusual about your home?

B **Write a description of your dream home. Use the model and your answers from Part A to help you.**

C PAIR WORK **Share your writing. Ask and answer questions for more information.**

My Dream Home

My dream home is on the beach in Hawaii. It's a very big house. It has five bedrooms, five bathrooms, and a lot of light and space. There are two kitchens. One kitchen is inside the house. The other kitchen is outside because we have a lot of barbecues on the beach!

A: What color is the house?

B: It's white.

A: What is your favorite part of the house?

B: The swimming pool.

I can describe a home. ✓

Wrap-up

1 Quick pair review

Lesson A Brainstorm!

Make a list of the rooms in a house and the things that go in each room. How many do you know? You have two minutes.

Lesson B Do you remember?

Complete the conversations with the correct words. You have two minutes.

1 A Could __________ you turn down the music, please?
  B No p__________.

2 A W__________ you answer the phone, please?
  B I'd be h__________ to.

3 A Could you buy some milk, p__________?
  B S__________.

Lesson C Test your partner!

Act out a chore. Can your partner guess what it is? Take turns. You and your partner have two minutes.

Lesson D Guess!

Describe a room in your house, but don't say its name. Can your partner guess what room it is? Take turns.
You and your partner have two minutes.

A: *This is my favorite room. There are three posters on the wall.*

B: *Is it your bedroom?*

A: *Yes, it is.*

2 In the real world

Go online and find information in English about an unusual house. Then write about it.

- Why is it unusual?
- What are the rooms like?
- Find a picture of the home, if possible.

An Unusual Home

Fallingwater is a famous house at the top of a waterfall. It has rooms that look like ...

Answers to Warm-up Part A (page 35)
a. Japan **b.** Iceland **c.** Brazil **d.** France

5 Health

LESSON A
- Parts of the body
- Imperatives; adverbs of manner

LESSON B
- Saying how you feel
- Wishing someone well

LESSON C
- Healthy habits
- *How* questions

LESSON D
- Reading: "Feeling Stressed?"
- Writing: Managing stress

Warm Up

A Describe the pictures. Which activities are good for you? Which ones aren't?

B Do you ever do any of the things in the pictures? Which ones?

A Breathe deeply.

1 Vocabulary Parts of the body

A Label the pictures with the correct words. Then listen and check your answers.

a arm	d finger	g head	j mouth	m shoulder
b ear	e foot (feet)	h knee	k neck	n stomach
c eye	f hand	i leg	l nose	o wrist

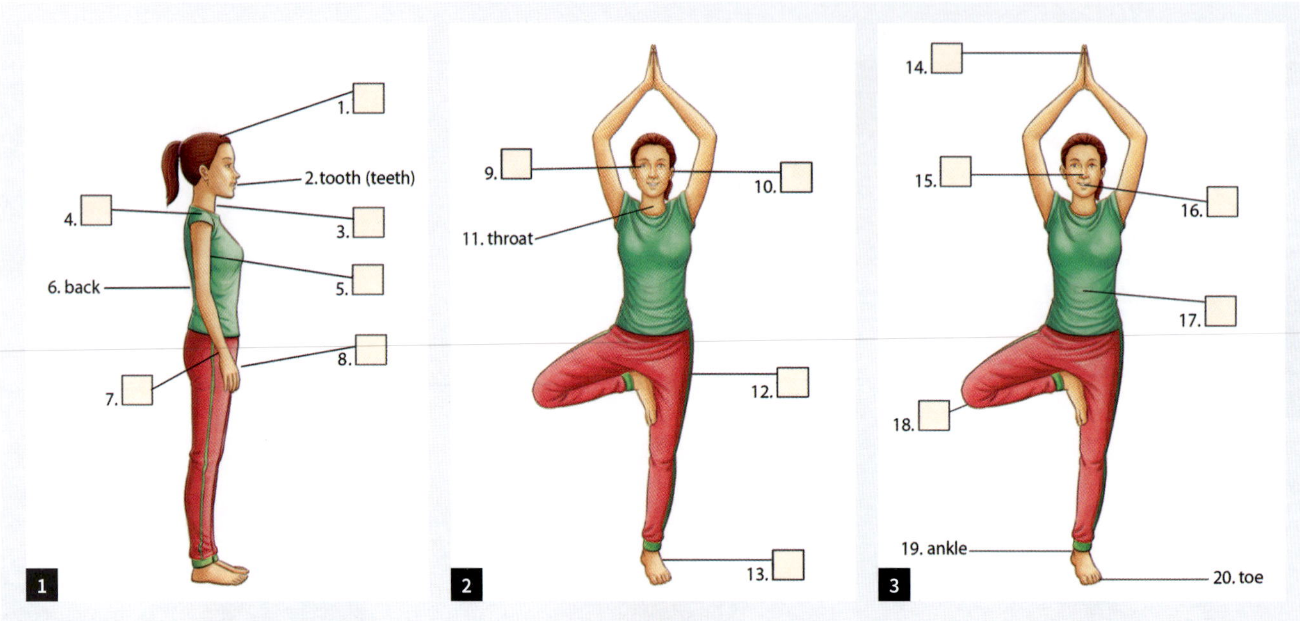

B PAIR WORK Point to a part of your body. Your partner names it. Take turns.

"That's your arm. And those are your ears."

2 Language in context Yoga for beginners

A Match the exercises with the yoga pictures in Exercise 1. Listen and check your answers.

A. ______ Place your right foot carefully on your left leg. Stretch your arms over your head. Hold for 30 seconds. Lower your arms and foot slowly.

B. ______ Repeat on the other side. Place your left foot carefully on your right leg. Stretch your arms over your head. Hold for 30 seconds.

C. ______ Stand up. Hold your stomach in. Keep your back and neck straight. Relax your arms. Don't hold your breath. Breathe slowly and deeply.

B What about you? Do you do yoga? If not, would you like to try it? Why or why not?

3 Grammar Imperatives; adverbs of manner

Breathe slowly and deeply.	**Don't breathe** quickly.
Stretch your arms.	**Don't relax** your arms.
Hold for 30 seconds.	**Don't hold** your breath.
Repeat on the other side.	**Don't repeat** on the other side.

Adjective	Adverb
slow	slow**ly**
careful	careful**ly**
deep	deep**ly**
noisy	nois**ily**

A Complete these exercise tips with the correct imperative form. Then compare with a partner.

✓do drink eat exercise find stretch

1 __Don't do__ too much the first day!
2 ______ your body for a few minutes.
3 ______ a place with a lot of space.
4 ______ some water.
5 ______ a big meal before you exercise.
6 ______ twice a week.

B Circle the correct adverbs. Then compare with a partner.

1 Walk **quickly** / **slowly** for 20 minutes every day.
2 Eat **quickly** / **slowly** at every meal.
3 Breathe **heavily** / **deeply** when you exercise.
4 Sit **quietly** / **noisily** for a few minutes each day.
5 Stretch **carefully** / **heavily** every morning.

4 Pronunciation Reduction of *and*

Listen and repeat. Notice how *and* is pronounced /ən/ before some consonant sounds.

Breathe slowly and (/ən/) deeply. Keep your back and (/ən/) neck straight.

5 Speaking Lower your arms slowly.

PAIR WORK Make sentences with the words below. Your partner does the actions. Take turns.

"Point to your nose slowly."

A		B	C
Stretch Lower Point to Move Raise Touch	your	arms hand head leg nose toes	slowly. carefully. quickly. to the right / left. up and down.

6 Keep talking!

Go to page 135 for more practice.

I can give and follow instructions.

B I'm not feeling well.

1 Health problems

Listen. Then act out a health problem. Your partner guesses it.

a backache

a cold

a cough

an earache

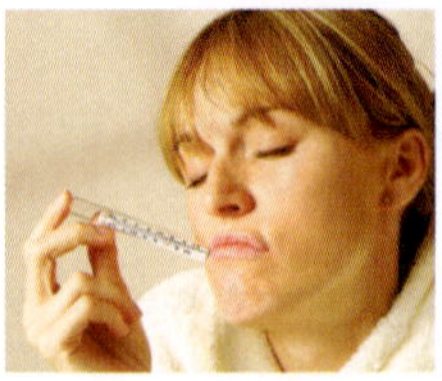
a fever

the flu

a headache

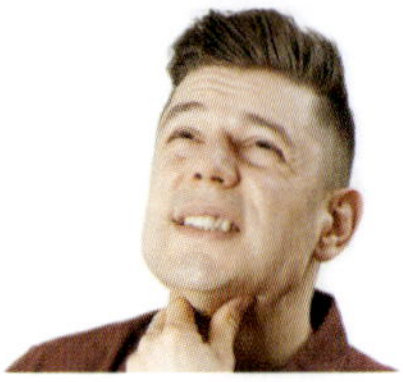
a sore throat

a stomachache

a toothache

"Do you have a cold?"

2 Interactions When you're not feeling well

A Listen to the conversation. What's wrong with Margaret? Then practice the conversation.

Debbie Hey, Margaret. How are you?

Margaret I'm not feeling well.

Debbie Oh? What's wrong?

Margaret I have a headache. I think I'd like to go home and rest.

Debbie That's fine. Take it easy.

B Listen to the expressions. Then practice the conversation again with the new expressions.

Saying how you feel

I'm not feeling well. | I don't feel so good. | I feel awful.

Wishing someone well

Take it easy. | Get well soon. | I hope you feel better.

3 Listening What's wrong?

A Listen to four phone conversations. Number the pictures from 1 to 4.

B Listen again. How does each caller wish the person well? Write the expression.

1 ______________________ 3 ______________________

2 ______________________ 4 ______________________

4 Speaking We're not feeling well.

CLASS ACTIVITY **Role-play these situations. Then change roles.**

Group A: Walk around the class and ask people in Group B how they feel. Use expressions from Exercise 2.

Group B: Imagine you have a health problem. Tell the people in Group A about it. Use expressions from Exercise 2.

A: How are you?

B: I don't feel so good.

A: Oh? What's wrong?

B: I have a stomachache.

A: I'm sorry to hear that. I hope you feel better.

I can wish someone well.

C How healthy are you?

1 Vocabulary Healthy habits

A Complete the phrases with the correct verbs. Then listen and check your answers.

eat	eat	exercise	get	go	lift	protect	wash

1 ________ a balanced diet

2 ________ your hands

3 ________ your skin

4 ________ weights

5 ________ for a walk

6 ________ daily

7 ________ enough sleep

8 ________ a good breakfast

B PAIR WORK **Which of the healthy habits in Part A do you have? Tell your partner.**

2 Conversation I don't have much energy.

A Listen and practice.

Laura What's wrong, Hal? Are you OK?

Hal Oh, hi, Laura. I don't know. I just don't have much energy.

Laura Hmm. Do you eat breakfast every day?

Hal Sure. And I exercise. I lift weights at my gym.

Laura And how often do you go there?

Hal Three or four days a week.

Laura That's not bad. How long do you spend there?

Hal Oh, about an hour a day.

Laura That's good. And how much sleep do you get?

Hal Quite a bit, about ten hours a night.

Laura Ten hours? That's why you don't have any energy. I think that's too much sleep!

B Listen to the rest of the conversation. What else does Laura ask about?

3 Grammar How questions

How often do you go to the gym?
Three or four days a week.

How long do you spend at the gym?
About an hour.

How well do you follow your diet?
Not very well.

How healthy are your eating habits?
Somewhat healthy.

How many meals do you eat a day?
Five small meals.

How much sleep do you get?
Quite a bit.

A Complete the questions with a *How* question. Then compare with a partner.

1 ____________________ do you protect your skin from the sun?
  a Extremely well. b Pretty well. c Not very well.

2 ____________________ are your eating habits?
  a Very healthy. b Quite healthy. c Not healthy at all.

3 ____________________ coffee do you drink in a week?
  a A lot. b Quite a bit. c Not much.

4 ____________________ do you eat red meat?
  a Every day. b Several times a week. c Never.

5 ____________________ do you spend on the computer every week?
  a 40 hours. b 20 hours. c Five hours.

6 ____________________ times a day do you wash your hands?
  a About six times. b About three times. c Once.

B PAIR WORK Ask and answer the questions in Part A. Circle your partner's answers.

A: *How well do you protect your skin from the sun?*
B: *Not very well. I sometimes wear a hat, but I rarely use sunscreen.*

4 Speaking Good question!

A GROUP WORK Look at the pictures. How many different *How* questions can you make for each picture? Ask the questions.

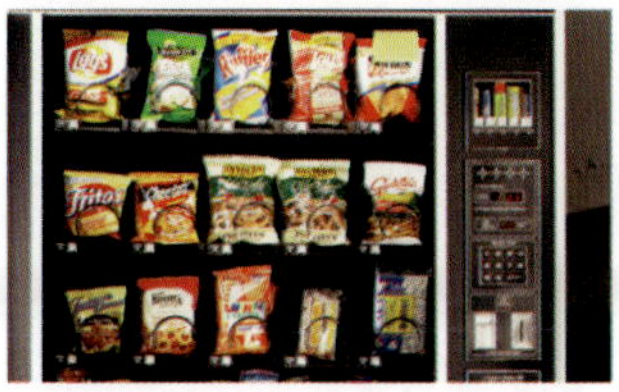

A: *How many times a week do you lift weights?*
B: *Never. I go to the gym once a week, but I don't lift weights.*
C: *How long do you spend at the gym?*

B How healthy do you think you are?

5 Keep talking!

Go to page 136 for more practice.

I can ask and talk about healthy habits.

D Don't stress out!

1 Reading

A Read the article. Write the correct headings above the paragraphs.

Communicate	Breathe	Do Nothing	Move!	Laugh	Get Organized

FEELING STRESSED?

Everyone feels stress, and a little stress is OK. It's what gives you energy and pushes you to do well at school or work. But too much stress is not good. There are ways to manage stress. Try one or more of these tips the next time you feel stressed out.

1. ______________

Take a deep breath. Breathe slowly and deeply every time you begin to feel stress. Make this a habit, and you can often stop a little stress from becoming a lot of stress.

2. ______________

Make a "to do" list, and decide what you need to do right away and what can easily wait. Clean up your study or work space. Do the same with your computer desktop.

3. ______________

Go for a swim. Run. Ride your bicycle. Do aerobics. Hike up a mountain. It doesn't really matter what you do. Just do something that you enjoy.

4. ______________

Have a problem? Don't keep it inside. Talk to a friend, a family member, or even your cat. Don't want to talk? Write it down in a stress journal.

5. ______________

See a funny movie. Tell some jokes. Watch some silly pet videos on the Internet. Laughter – yours or someone else's – is often the best medicine.

6. ______________

That's right . . . nothing. Close the door. No TV, computer, or phone. Sit down and take a break from life. Close your eyes, and feel the stress . . . disappear.

B Read the article again. Write the tip next to what each person does to manage stress.

______	Jill	I watch my favorite TV show, and I laugh and laugh.
______	Rachid	I go jogging. It makes me feel better.
______	Paul	I just sit quietly. That's all I do!
______	Valerie	I clean my house and put everything away.
______	Ming	I stop and breathe deeply.
______	Eduardo	I call a good friend and talk for a while.

C PAIR WORK Which tips in Part A do you think work? Tell your partner.

2 Listening It works for me!

A 🎧 **Listen to four people talk about how they manage stress. What do they do? Number the pictures from 1 to 4. There are two extra items.**

☐ 

☐ 

☐ 

☐ 

☐ 

☐ 

B 🎧 **Listen again. What else do the people do to manage stress? Write the activities.**

1 ____________________ 3 ____________________

2 ____________________ 4 ____________________

3 Writing Managing stress

A Think about how you manage stress. Answer the questions.

- How much stress do you feel?
- What makes you stressed?
- How well do you manage stress?
- What do you do?

B Write a paragraph about how you manage stress. Use the model and your answers in Part A to help you.

C PAIR WORK **Share your writing. Do the same things stress you out?**

How I Manage Stress

I don't often feel stressed, but Mondays are sometimes difficult. I'm a full-time student, but I have a part-time job on Mondays. Here are a few ways I manage stress on Mondays. I eat a good breakfast and lift weights. Then I go to school early and talk with friends. It really helps.

4 Speaking Living with stress

PAIR WORK **Imagine you are one of these people. Ask your partner for tips to help you manage your stress.**

- A mother with two young children and no time
- A young man before his wedding
- A soccer player before a big game
- A student before a big test

A: I'm very tired and my children never stop. What can I do?

B: Talk to your friends and find out what they do.

I can discuss ways to manage stress. ✓

Wrap-up

1 Quick pair review

Lesson A **Test your partner!**

Say the name of a sport. Can your partner say what parts of the body you use for the sport? Take turns. You have one minute.

A: *Soccer.*

B: *Legs, feet, head, . . .*

Lesson B **Brainstorm!**

Make a list of ways to say how you feel and ways to wish someone well. You have two minutes.

Lesson C **Do you remember?**

Complete the questions with *much*, *well*, *healthy*, *many*, and *long*. You have one minute.

1 How ______________ apples do you eat a week?

2 How ______________ stress do you have at work?

3 How ______________ do you work on Saturdays?

4 How ______________ is your lifestyle?

5 How ______________ do you manage stress?

Lesson D **Guess!**

Act out a way to manage stress. Can your partner guess what it is? Take turns. You have one minute.

A: *Are you exercising?*

B: *Yes, I am.*

2 In the real world

What other ways can you manage stress? Go online and find three ideas in English. Then write about them.

Three Ways to Manage Stress

Turn off your computer and your phone for an hour. Then turn on some relaxing music. Open a good book . . .

6 What's on TV?

LESSON A
- Types of TV shows
- Verb + infinitive or gerund

LESSON B
- Agreeing with an opinion
- Disagreeing with an opinion

LESSON C
- Television
- Present continuous for future plans

LESSON D
- Reading: "Reality Shows"
- Writing: My favorite TV show

Warm Up

A Match the words with TV shows in the online menu.

a exciting b funny c serious d sad

B Can you name some TV shows from your country? What kinds of TV shows do you like to watch?

A I love watching game shows.

1 Vocabulary Types of TV shows

A Match the TV shows and the pictures. Then listen and check your answers.

a a cartoon
b a documentary
c a drama
d a game show
e the news
f a reality show
g a sitcom
h a soap opera
i a talk show

1 

2 

3 

4 

5 

6 

7 

8 

9 

B PAIR WORK What was the last show you watched on TV? What type of show was it? Tell your partner.

"I watched a sitcom with my parents. It was . . ."

2 Language in context TV preferences

A Listen to four people talk about their TV preferences. Who doesn't watch TV very much?

I watch a lot of TV. I really enjoy baseball. And I hope to get a big new TV soon.

– Jessica

I love soap operas. My favorite is *Our Life*. I like seeing my favorite actors.

– Lucas

I don't like reality shows at all. I love to watch documentaries and game shows.

– Gustavo

I hardly ever watch TV. I prefer to listen to the radio. I hate to miss the news.

– Min-hwa

B Which person in Part A are you similar to?

3 Grammar Verb + infinitive or gerund

Verb + infinitive	Verb + infinitive or gerund
I **hope to get** a big TV.	I **like to see** / **seeing** my favorite actors.
I **want to see** every baseball game.	I **love to watch** / **watching** game shows.
Verb + gerund	I **prefer to listen** / **listening** to the radio.
I **enjoy watching** football games.	I **hate to miss** / **missing** the news.
I **dislike watching** TV.	

A Circle the correct verb forms. If both forms are correct, circle both. Then practice with a partner.

1 A What types of TV shows do you like **to watch** / **watching** late at night?
  B Actually, I dislike **to watch** / **watching** TV at night. I prefer **to be** / **being** online.

2 A What do you want **to watch** / **watching** on TV tonight? A reality show?
  B I hate **to watch** / **watching** those shows. I enjoy **to watch** / **watching** dramas.

3 A Do you want **to see** / **seeing** a movie tonight?
  B No, not tonight. My favorite TV show is on, and I hate **to miss** / **missing** it.

B Complete the questions with a correct form of the verb. Then compare with a partner.

1 Do you enjoy ________________ (watch) cartoons on TV?
2 What do you want ________________ (watch) on TV this weekend?
3 Do you like ________________ (guess) the answers on game shows?
4 What types of TV shows do you dislike ________________ (watch)?

C PAIR WORK **Ask and answer the questions in Part B. Answer with your own information.**

4 Speaking TV Talk

A Add one more thing to the chart.

Find someone who . . .	Name
1 enjoys watching documentaries	
2 wants to buy a new TV	
3 hopes to meet a famous actress or actor	
4 hates missing soap operas	
5	

B CLASS ACTIVITY **Find a classmate for each sentence. Write their names.**

A: *Do you enjoy watching documentaries?*
B: *Yes, I do.*

5 Keep talking!

Go to page 137 for more practice.

I can talk about types of TV shows I like.

B I don't really agree.

1 Interactions Agreeing and disagreeing

A Look at the picture. What are the people doing? Do you think they like the TV show?

B Listen to the conversation. Why doesn't Vasco like talk shows? Then practice the conversation.

Fred Let's see what's on TV. . . .Oh, no! I don't like this talk show at all. I think it's terrible.

Vasco I agree. Actually, I hate all talk shows. I think they're really boring.

Fred Really? I disagree. I think some of them are pretty interesting.

Vasco I don't think any talk shows are interesting.

Fred Well, would you like to watch something else?

C Listen to the expressions. Then practice the conversation again with the new expressions.

Agreeing with an opinion		
I agree.	I agree with you.	I think so, too.

Disagreeing with an opinion		
I disagree.	I don't really agree.	I'm afraid I disagree.

D Complete each response with one of the expressions from Part C. Then practice with a partner.

1 A Most TV sitcoms are funny. B ______ I never laugh at them.
2 A Reality shows are great. B ______ I watch them all the time.
3 A Game shows are exciting. B ______ I think they're boring.
4 A It's good to watch the news. B ______ I watch it every night.
5 A Cartoons are just for children. B ______ They're for adults, too.

2 Listening What else is on?

A 🎧 **Listen to Dan and Amy discuss what is on TV. Number the TV shows from 1 to 5. (There is one extra picture.)**

B 🎧 **Listen again. Look at Amy's opinion of each show. Write Dan's opinion.**

Amy's opinions:	Dan's opinions:
1 boring	1 ______
2 great	2 ______
3 interesting	3 ______
4 exciting	4 ______
5 fantastic	5 ______

3 Speaking My opinion

A **Check (✓) the statements you agree with. Then make the statements you disagree with true for you.**

- ☐ Documentaries are ~~boring.~~ exciting
- ☐ Talk shows are very interesting.
- ☐ All sports programs are exciting.
- ☐ Most sitcoms are very funny.
- ☐ It's important to watch the TV news.
- ☐ Reality shows are boring.

B GROUP WORK **Share your ideas.**

A: *In my opinion, documentaries are exciting.*

B: *I don't really agree. I think they're pretty boring.*

C: *What about talk shows? I think they're very interesting.*

A: *I agree with you.*

I can agree and disagree with an opinion. ✓

C I'm recording a documentary.

1 Vocabulary Television

A Match the words and the definitions. Then listen and check your answers.

1 I often **record** my favorite show. C
2 I often **fast-forward** through the boring parts of shows. ____
3 I always **skip** the sad parts of movies. ____
4 I watch **reruns** of old sitcoms. ____
5 I never lose the **remote control**. ____
6 Most **commercials** are funny. ____
7 You can learn a lot from **public TV**. ____
8 I think **satellite TV** is great. ____

a to play a show at high speed
b to not watch something
c to store a show to watch it later
d advertisements for products
e a nonprofit TV network
f a service that sends TV shows to homes through a dish
g repeat showings of a TV show
h a device used to control a TV from a distance

B PAIR WORK **Which sentences in Part A describe your opinions or habits? Tell your partner.**

A: *I often record my favorite show.*
B: *Really? I never record my favorite show.*

2 Conversation I'm going away this weekend.

A Listen and practice.

Nora Hi, Zack. How are you?
Zack Oh, hi, Nora. I'm fine. Actually, I'm going away this weekend, so I want to record some TV shows.
Nora Really? Which shows?
Zack On Friday night, I'm recording the soccer game. The Hawks are playing the Lions.
Nora Oh, I'm watching that at Lisa's. She's having a soccer party. She has satellite TV now.
Zack Well, I'm watching it on Sunday night. That way I can fast-forward and skip the commercials.
Nora Good idea. I hate watching commercials. So what else are you recording?
Zack On Saturday, I'm recording a documentary on Channel 11 called *TV Is Dead*.

B Listen to the rest of the conversation. **What is Nora watching on TV this weekend?**

3 Grammar Present continuous for future plans

I'm **recording** the soccer game.	**Is** Zack **watching** the game on Sunday?
I'**m not recording** the sitcom.	Yes, he **is**. No, he'**s not**. / No, he **isn't**.
She'**s having** a soccer party this week.	**Are** they **watching** the game on Sunday?
She'**s not visiting** her family.	Yes, they **are**. No, they'**re not**. / No, they **aren't**.
They'**re playing** the Lions this weekend.	What else **are** you **recording** on Friday?
They'**re not playing** the Sharks.	I'**m** also **recording** a movie.

A Complete these conversations with the present continuous form of the verbs. Then practice with a partner.

1 A What ________ you ________ (do) this weekend? ________ you ________ (go) anywhere?

B No, I ________ (stay) home all weekend. Some friends ________ (come) over to watch a basketball game. The Tigers ________ (play).

2 A I ________ (get) satellite TV on Wednesday – finally! What ________ you ________ (do) on Friday? Do you want to come over?

B I'd love to, but I can't. Joe and I ________ (visit) his parents this weekend. We ________ (leave) on Friday after work.

B What are you doing this weekend? Use these verbs to write about your weekend plans. Then tell your partner.

1 (meet) ________
2 (watch) ________
3 (play) ________
4 (go out) ________

4 Pronunciation Sentence stress

Listen and repeat. Notice how the important words in a sentence are stressed.

I'm **going** to **Colombia** on **Monday**. She's **staying home** this **weekend**.

5 Speaking What are you recording?

A Imagine you are going away next week, and you can't watch TV. Decide where you're going and make a list of five shows you are recording.

B CLASS ACTIVITY **Compare lists. Is anyone recording the same shows? Find classmates with a similar list.**

A: *I'm visiting my mother next Tuesday, so I'm recording . . .*

B: *Me, too. I love . . ., and I'm recording . . .*

6 Keep talking!

Go to page 138 for more practice.

I can describe future plans.

D Popular TV

1 Reading

A Read the article. Match the headings to the descriptions of the reality shows.

a Improvement shows b Game-style shows c Documentary-style shows

REALITY SHOWS

You either love them or you hate them! But did you realize there are different types of reality shows? Read on and find out more. . .

In this type of reality show, **contestants** try to win a prize. The prize is often money or, in some cases, a job. Each week, one person leaves the show until there is only one – the winner. Sometimes the contestants vote on who stays or goes, sometimes the TV **viewers** at home vote, and other times the show's **judges** choose. One example is *Master Chef*. In this show, contestants cook dishes for the **host** and the three judges. The winner usually receives money, a course, and a trophy.

This type of reality show looks like a soap opera, but it is about one or more real people and their daily lives. Some of the shows are about people on the job, such as police officers, firefighters, or hospital workers. Others are about regular people in unusual situations, and some even follow famous people. One example of this type is *Keeping Up with the Kardashians*. This show is about the daily life of the Kardashian family in Los Angeles, CA. In these types of shows, there is no prize money and no winner.

These shows are about a person or people who need a change. Other people help this person in one area, such as home, style, health, or relationships. An example of this is *The Property Brothers*. On each show, identical twin brothers help a couple buy and transform an inexpensive house into their dream home. The couple needs to help with the transformation and stay on budget.

B Read the article again. Look at the questions. Check (✓) the correct answer.

Which show . . .?	Master Chef	Keeping Up with the Kardashians	The Property Brothers
has a host	☐	☐	☐
gives a trophy	☐	☐	☐
shows people's daily lives	☐	☐	☐
is about home improvement	☐	☐	☐
is like a soap opera	☐	☐	☐

C Find the words in bold in the article. What do they mean? Match the definitions and the correct word.

A person / People who . . .

a presents a TV show ______________

b participate in a competition ______________

c watch a television program ______________

d decide who wins or loses ______________

D PAIR WORK **Imagine you can be on one type of reality show. Which would you choose? Why? Tell your partner.**

2 Listening Favorite shows back home

A Listen to three students talk about their favorite TV shows in their countries. What type of show does each like? Write it in the chart.

	Type of show	Favorite thing about the show	
Valerie		the models	the end of each show
Young-ho		the costumes	the actors
Claudia		the teenagers	the stories

B Listen again. What is their favorite thing about the show? Circle the correct answers.

3 Writing My favorite TV show

A Think of your favorite TV show. Answer the questions.

- What type of show is it?
- What happens on the show?
- Why do you enjoy watching it?
- Is there anything you don't like about it?

My Favorite TV Show

I like to watch the reality show "Project Runway." The contestants are fashion students. The winner receives money and an article in a fashion magazine. I enjoy watching the show because the clothes are fantastic, but sometimes I disagree with the judges.

B Write a paragraph about your favorite TV show. Use the model and your answers in Part A to help you.

C GROUP WORK Share your writing. Do you agree with each other's opinions?

4 Speaking Reality shows

A GROUP WORK Read about these reality shows. Which ones sound interesting? Why?

The Amazing Race
the U.S.
Pairs race one another around the world. The winners receive a million dollars.

The Genius Game
South Korea
Reality-style game show where contestants compete to solve logic puzzles and games.

The Grand Tour
the U.K.
Three British men drive a variety of motor vehicles on adventures around the world.

B Do you ever watch similar shows in your country? Why or why not?

"I watch a show similar to *The Amazing Race*. I don't really like it, but I always watch it!"

I can give my opinions about popular TV shows.

Wrap-up

1 Quick pair review

Lesson A **Brainstorm!**

Make a list of types of TV shows. How many do you remember? You have one minute.

Lesson B **Do you remember?**

Write *A* for expressions that show you agree with an opinion. Write *D* for expressions that show you disagree. You have one minute.

1 I disagree. ______
2 I think so, too. ______
3 I agree. ______
4 I don't really agree. ______
5 I'm afraid I disagree. ______
6 I agree with you. ______

Lesson C **Find out!**

What are three things both you and your partner are doing next week? Take turns. You and your partner have two minutes.

A: *I'm watching a baseball game next week. Are you?*

B: *Yes, I am.*

Lesson D **Guess!**

Describe your favorite TV show, but don't say its name. Can your partner guess the name and type of show it is? Take turns. You and your partner have two minutes.

A: In this TV show, celebrities dance with professional dancers.

B: Is it a reality show?

A: Yes, it is.

B: Is it *Dancing with the Stars*?

A: Yes, it is.

2 In the real world

What new shows are on TV this year? Look at a TV schedule or go online and find information about a new TV show in English. Then write about it.

- What's the name of the TV show?
- What type of TV show is it?
- What's it about?
- When is it on?

A New TV Show

"The Crown" is a drama.
It's about the life of Queen
Elizabeth II of the U.K.

Answers to Warm-up, Part A:
1. e 2007 **2.** b 1994 **3.** c 1999 **4.** f 2009 **5.** d 2002 **6.** a 1989

7 Shopping

LESSON A

- Opposites
- Comparative adjectives

LESSON B

- Bargaining for a lower price
- Suggesting a different price

LESSON C

- Adjectives to describe clothing
- *Enough* and *too*

LESSON D

- Reading: "Chatuchak Weekend Market"
- Writing: An interesting market

Warm up

A Describe the pictures. How many things can you name?

B Where do you usually shop? What do you like to buy?

A It's lighter and thinner.

1 Vocabulary Opposites

A Label the pictures with the correct words. Then listen and check your answers.

big	expensive	heavy	loud	slow	thick

small ________

quiet ________

thin ________

light ________

fast ________

cheap ________

B PAIR WORK Use the words in Part A to describe things you own. Tell your partner.

"My cell phone is thin and light."

2 Language in context Which is better?

A Read the message board. Then label the pictures.

Group posts

Topic: **Star X07 or MyPhone**

michael12 Posted May 5 11:45 p.m.
Help! I need a phone and can't decide between the Star X07 or the MyPhone. Which is better?

johnnyjay Posted May 6 8:07 a.m.
Get the Star X07. It's lighter and thinner than the MyPhone.

cybergal Posted May 6 9:52 p.m.
The MyPhone is better. It's less expensive, and the Internet connection is faster. It has a larger choice of colors, too. The Star X07 only comes in black.

____

____

B Which of the two phones do you like?

3 Grammar Comparative adjectives

The Star X07 is **lighter than** the MyPhone.
The MyPhone is **heavier than** the Star X07.
Which cell phone is **more expensive**?
The Star X07 is **more expensive than** the MyPhone.
The MyPhone is **less expensive than** the Star X07.
Is the MyPhone **better than** the Star X07?
No, I don't think it's **better**. It's **worse**.

Adjective	Comparative
light	lighter
nice	nicer
thin	thinner
heavy	heavier
difficult	more / less difficult
good	better
bad	worse

Complete the sentences with the correct comparative form. Add *than* if necessary. Then compare with a partner.

1 Is your new printer ________________ (fast) your old one?
2 Are desktop computers always ________________ (heavy) laptops?
3 This new camera is really cheap! It's ________________ (expensive) than my old one.
4 I like this TV, but I think I want a ________________ (big) one.
5 This phone has a big screen, so it's ________________ (expensive) than other phones.
6 My new camera isn't ________________ (good) my old one. In fact, it's ________________ (bad)!

4 Speaking Let's compare

A PAIR WORK **Compare these products. How many sentences can you make?**

Car A

Watch A
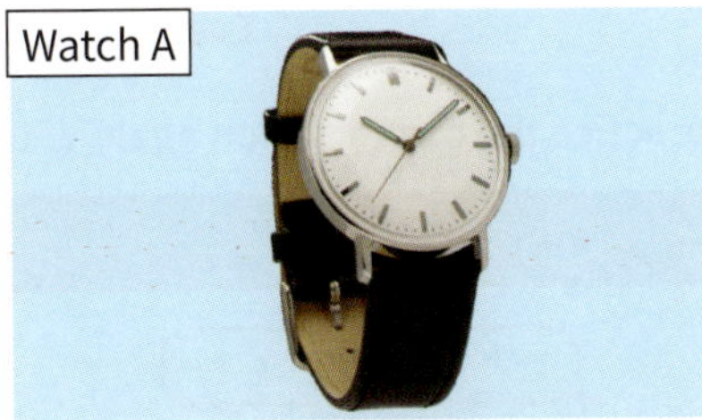
Camera A

Car B

Watch B

Camera B

A: *Car A is older than Car B.*
B: *And it's slower. Do you think Car A is quieter?*

B PAIR WORK **Which product in each pair do you prefer? Why?**

5 Keep talking!

Go to page 139 for more practice.

I can describe and compare products.

B Would you take $10?

1 Interactions Bargaining

A Do you ever bargain for lower prices? Where? For what? Do you enjoy bargaining?

B Listen to the conversation. Does Eve buy the lamp? Then practice the conversation.

Eve Excuse me. How much is this lamp?
Rob Oh, it's only $20.
Eve Wow, that's expensive! How about $10?
Rob No, I'm sorry. $20 is a good price.
Eve Well, thanks anyway.
Rob Wait! You can have it for $15.
Eve $15? OK. I'll take it.

C Listen to the expressions. Then practice the conversation again with the new expressions.

Bargaining for a lower price

- How about . . .?
- Will you take . . . ?
- Would you take . . .?

Suggesting a different price

- You can have it / them for . . .
- I'll let you have it / them for . . .
- I'll give it / them to you for . . .

D Number the sentences from 1 to 7. Then practice with a partner.

_____ **A** I'll take them. Thank you very much.
_____ **A** $30? That's pretty expensive. Would you take $20?
_____ **A** OK. Well, thank you anyway.
_____ **A** Excuse me. How much are these earrings?
_____ **B** Just a moment. I'll give them to you for $25.
_____ **B** No, I'm sorry. $30 is the price.
_____ **B** They're only $30.

2 Pronunciation Linked sounds

A Listen and repeat. Notice how final consonant sounds are often linked to the vowel sounds that follow them.

How much is this lamp? It's only $20.

B Listen and mark the linked sounds. Then practice with a partner.

1 How much are the earrings? 2 Just a moment. 3 Thanks anyway.

3 Listening How much is it?

A Listen to four people shopping at a yard sale. Number the pictures from 1 to 4. (There is one extra picture.)

$ ______

$ ______

$ ______

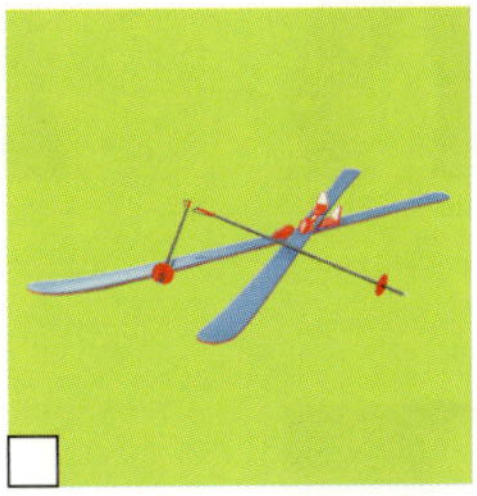
$ ______

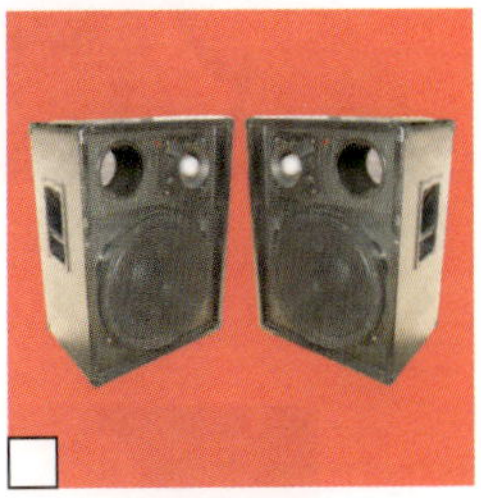
$ ______

B Listen again. Write the price the buyer and seller agree on.

4 Speaking What a bargain!

A Write the prices on the tags.

B PAIR WORK Role-play the situations. Then change roles.

Student A: Sell the things. You want to sell them for a good price.

Student B: Buy the things. Bargain for lower prices.

A: *Excuse me. How much is the computer?*

B: *It's only $250.*

A: *That's very expensive. Would you take . . .?*

I can bargain.

C This hat is too small.

1 Vocabulary Adjectives to describe clothing

A Complete the phrases with the correct words. Then listen and check your answers.

baggy	comfortable	pretty	ugly
bright	plain	tight	uncomfortable

1 a ________ shirt

2 ________ jeans

3 ________ shoes

4 a ________ blouse

5 a ________ tie

6 a ________ dress

7 ________ pants

8 an ________ hat

B PAIR WORK **Describe your clothing today. Tell your partner.**

"I think my shirt is plain, but comfortable. My jeans are a little baggy."

2 Conversation Try it on!

A Listen and practice.

Allie Let's look at the jackets.

Paul OK, but I have a class at 3:00. Do we have enough time?

Allie Sure. It's only 1:30. Hey! Look at this black one.

Paul It's cool. Try it on.

Allie OK. What do you think? Does it fit?

Paul No, it's too small. Try this red one.

Allie OK. How does it look? Is it big enough?

Paul I think so. Yeah, it looks good on you.

Allie How much is it? Can you see the tag?

Paul Let's see . . . it's $120.

Allie Oh, no! I only have $60. I don't have enough money. I can't afford it.

B Listen to the rest of the conversation. What else does Allie try on?

3 Grammar *Enough and too*

Enough *means the right amount.* Too *means more than enough.*

Enough *before nouns*

I have **enough** time.

I don't have **enough** money.

Enough *after adjectives*

The jacket is big **enough**.

The pants aren't long **enough**.

Too *before adjectives*

The jacket is **too** small.

The pants aren't **too** long.

A Complete the sentences with the correct words. Use *too* and *enough*. Then compare with a partner.

big	✓ long	money	uncomfortable

1 How do these pants look? Do you think they're long enough ?
2 These shoes look nice, but they're ________________. I can't walk at all.
3 Oh, no! I don't have ________________. This belt is $30, and I only have $20.
4 The shirt I ordered online is ________________. It fits very well.

B Rewrite the sentences. Use *enough* and *too*. Then compare with a partner.

1 Those boots are too small. (enough) These boots aren't big enough.
2 That belt is $10. I have $10. (enough) ________________
3 The jacket is expensive. I can't afford it. (too) ________________
4 That belt is $12. I have $10. (enough) ________________
5 I wear a large size. This T-shirt isn't big enough. (too) ________________
6 These pants aren't long enough. (too) ________________

4 Speaking Things I never wear

A Think of your closet at home. Complete the chart with pieces of clothing. Write reasons why you don't wear them.

Things I don't like wearing	Things I never wear
Ties – too ugly	

B GROUP WORK Share your ideas. What do you have in common?

5 Keep talking!

Student A go to page 140 and Student B go to page 144 for more practice.

I can describe how clothing looks and fits.

D A shopper's paradise

1 Reading

A **Read the webpage. Which paragraph includes information about these topics? Number the topics from 1 to 4.**

☐ transportation ☐ number of visitors ☐ prices and money ☐ hours

CHATUCHAK WEEKEND MARKET

1 With more than 15,000 shops and 200,000 visitors every Saturday and Sunday, Bangkok's Chatuchak Weekend Market is a popular place with visitors to Thailand. You can find plants, flowers, music, jewelry, clothes, food, and even animals!

2 The market is a great place to find bargains, and prices are **generally** low. Most people bargain, but some don't, so don't worry if you don't want to bargain. Just go with a friendly smile and have enough cash in your pocket. There are ATMs for cash, but they are difficult to find, and many **vendors** don't take credit cards. The market is **huge**, and many people walk in circles, even with a map. Don't try to see it all in one day!

3 The market is open from 8:00 to 6:00 Saturday and Sunday. It's good to get there early, before it gets too busy. Wear light, comfortable clothing and bring a bottle of water. And for lunch, try some of Thailand's famous snacks, such as fried scorpions!

4 The market is very easy to get to. It's only a five-minute walk from Mo Chit station on Bangkok's Skytrain. Many people come by train but leave by taxi. It's easier to get your **purchases** back to your hotel that way!

B **Read the webpage again. Find the words in bold, and check (✓) the correct meaning.**

1 **generally** ☐ usually ☐ rarely

2 **vendors** ☐ buyers ☐ sellers

3 **huge** ☐ easy to find ☐ very large

4 **purchases** ☐ things you buy ☐ things you sell

C **Check (✓) the tips you think the writer would agree with.**

☐ Pay the first price the vendor offers.
☐ Arrive in the morning.
☐ Bring a credit card, not cash.
☐ Take the bus home after shopping.

D PAIR WORK **What would you like about Bangkok's Weekend Market? What wouldn't you like? Tell your partner.**

2 Listening Portobello Road Market

A Listen to two friends talk about Portobello Road Market. Answer the questions.

1 What city is the market in? ______
2 How many days is the outdoor market open? ______
3 When's a good time to visit? ______
4 What's a good way to get there? ______

B Listen again. What can you buy at the market on Saturday? Circle the words you hear.

animals cell phones clothes fruit jewelry meat vegetables

3 Writing An interesting market

A Think about a market you know. Answer the questions.

- What is the name of the market?
- Where is it?
- When is it open?
- When's a good time to visit?
- What can you buy there?

B Write a description of an interesting market. Use the model and your answers in Part A to help you.

The Farmers' Market is near my home. It's open every Saturday from 9:00 to 4:00. You can buy the best fruits and vegetables there. A good time to visit is late in the afternoon. It's not too busy then. You don't bargain at this market, but some vendors lower their prices at the end of the day.

C PAIR WORK Share your writing. How are the markets similar? How are they different?

4 Speaking A good place to shop

A Think about things you buy. Add two more things to the list. Then complete the rest of the chart.

Things I buy	Place	Reason
fruits and vegetables		
shoes		
old furniture		
computers and cell phones		

B GROUP WORK Share your ideas. Ask and answer questions for more information.

"I always go to the market to buy fruits and vegetables. They are always fresh, and the people are friendly."

I can discuss good places to shop.

Wrap-up

1 Quick pair review

Lesson A **Test your partner!**

Say an adjective. Can your partner say its opposite? Take turns. You have one minute.

A: *Small.*

B: *Big.*

Lesson B **Do you remember?**

Complete the conversation with the correct word. You have two minutes.

A How much is this TV?

B $50

A Will you ______________ (1) $30?

B You can ______________ (2) it for $45.

A How ______________ (3) $35?

B I'll ______________ (4) it to you for $40.

A OK.

Lesson C **Brainstorm!**

Make a list of adjectives to describe clothing. Take turns. You and your partner have two minutes.

Lesson D **Find out!**

What are two things both you and your partner buy at a market? Take turns. You and your partner have two minutes.

A: *I buy music at a market. Do you?*

B: *No, I don't. I buy music online.*

2 In the real world

What outdoor markets are famous? Go online and find information in English about an outdoor market. Then write about it.

- What's the name of the market?
- Where is it?
- When is it open?
- What do they sell at the market?

The Otavalo Market
The Otavalo M arket is in Ecuador. It's open every day, but Saturdays are very busy . . .

8 Fun in the city

LESSON A
- Places to see
- *Should; can*

LESSON B
- Asking for a recommendation
- Giving a recommendation

LESSON C
- Adjectives to describe cities
- Superlative adjectives

LESSON D
- Reading: "Austin or San Antonio?"
- Writing: A message board

1

2

3

4

5

6

Warm Up

A Describe the pictures. What is happening in each picture?

B Which of these things do you like about city life? Which don't you like?

A You shouldn't miss it!

1 Vocabulary Places to see

A Match the words and the pictures. Then listen and check your answers.

a botanical garden	c fountain	e palace	g square
b castle	d monument	f pyramid	h statue

1 ☐

2 ☐

3 ☐

4 ☐

5 ☐

6 ☐

7 ☐

8 ☐

B PAIR WORK **Which of the places in Part A do you have where you live? Discuss the places.**

"There's a nice statue in the center of the square."

2 Language in context Attractions in the city

A Read about what to do in these three cities. Which cities are good for shopping?

Guayaquil, Ecuador

Enjoy shopping, cafés, fountains, and statues on El Malecón, a popular walking area. It's a fantastic place to take a long, slow walk or ride on a tour boat.

Seoul, South Korea

You shouldn't miss the small neighborhood of Insadong. It's a great place to shop for books, pottery, and paintings. Later, you can walk to a nearby palace or relax at an old teahouse.

Cairo, Egypt

Love history? Then you should visit the Egyptian Museum. You can't see it all in one day, so be sure to see King Tut's treasure and the famous "mummy room."

B What about you? Which city in Part A would you like to visit? Why?

3 Grammar Should; can

Should for recommendations	*Can* for possibility
Where **should** I go? You **should** visit the Egyptian Museum. They **shouldn't** miss Insadong. (= They should see Insadong.) **Should** she go to Cairo? Yes, she **should**. No, she **shouldn't**.	What **can** I do there? You **can** enjoy cafés, shops, and fountains. You **can't** see all of the museum in one day. **Can** they take a taxi? Yes, they **can**. No, they **can't**.

Complete the conversation with *should*, *shouldn't*, *can*, or *can't*. Then practice with a partner.

A Should I rent a car in Seoul?

B No, I think you ________ take the subway. You ________ get around quickly and easily.

A Oh, good. And what places ________ I visit?

B Well, you ________ miss the palace, and you ________ also go to the art museum. You ________ see it all in one day because it's very big, but you ________ buy really nice art books and postcards there.

A OK. Thanks a lot!

4 Listening My city

A Listen to three people describe their cities. Number the pictures from 1 to 3.

Istanbul

1 ________
2 ________

Mexico City

1 ________
2 ________

Florence

1 ________
2 ________

B Listen again. Write two things the people say visitors should do in their cities.

5 Speaking Only one day

A PAIR WORK Imagine these people are planning to visit your town or city for only one day. What places should they visit?

- a family with teenage children
- a businessperson from overseas
- two college students
- young children on a school trip

"I think the family should visit the town square. They can eat and shop there."

B GROUP WORK Compare your answers from Part A. Do you agree?

6 Keep talking!

Go to page 142 for more practice.

I can say what people should do in a city.

B I'd recommend going . . .

1 Interactions Recommendations

A Look at the pictures. What do you think the woman is going to do soon?

B Listen to the conversation. Was your guess from Part A correct? Then practice the conversation.

Lucy Hi, Alex.

Alex Oh, hi, Lucy. Are you ready for your trip to Brazil?

Lucy Almost, but I don't really know much about Rio. What would you recommend doing there?

Alex I'd recommend going to a samba club.

Lucy A samba club? Really?

Alex Yeah. You can dance or just listen to the music. Everyone has a good time.

Lucy Great. That sounds fun!

C Listen to the expressions. Then practice the conversation again with the new expressions.

Asking for a recommendation

- What would you recommend doing there?
- What would you suggest doing there?
- What do you think I should do there?

Giving a recommendation

- I'd recommend going . . .
- I'd suggest going . . .
- I think you should go . . .

D Put the words in order. Then compare with a partner.

1. you / there / recommend / what / seeing / would ____________________?
2. I'd / the castle / visiting / suggest ____________________.
3. the square / I / should / think / you / go to ____________________.
4. suggest / would / doing / what / you / in Tokyo ____________________?
5. bus / recommend / I'd / the / taking ____________________.

2 Listening One day in Taipei

Listen to Carrie and David get information from the tourist information desk in Taipei. Check (✓) the recommendations you hear.

1 ☐ I'd suggest visiting Taipei 101.
☐ You should visit Taipei 101.

2 ☐ I'd recommend going to the night market.
☐ You shouldn't miss the night market.

3 ☐ I'd suggest going to the Fine Arts Museum.
☐ I'd recommend going to the Fine Arts Museum.

4 ☐ I think you should take the subway.
☐ I'd recommend taking the subway.

3 Speaking Role play

PAIR WORK **Role—play the situation. Then change roles.**

Student A: You are a tourist in London. Ask for recommendations for three things to do.

Student B: You work at a tourist information desk. Give recommendations for three things to do.

A: Hello. Can I help you?

B: Yes. This is my first time in London. What would you suggest doing here?

A: Well, there are a lot of things to do, but I think you should definitely visit the British Museum. You can see . . .

I can ask for and give a recommendation.

C The best and the worst

1 Vocabulary Adjectives to describe cities

A **Match the words and pictures. Then listen and check your answers.**

a beautiful	b dangerous	c dirty	d modern	e stressful

1 ☐

2 ☐

3 ☐

4 ☐

5 ☐

B **Write the opposites. Use the words in Part A. Then listen and check your answers.**

clean	relaxing	safe	traditional	ugly
dirty	______	______	______	______

C PAIR WORK **Describe where you live using the words in Parts A and B.**

"Our city is beautiful and clean, but life here can be stressful."

2 Conversation Life in Sydney

A **Listen and practice.**

Peter So, Akemi, how do you like living in Sydney?

Akemi I miss Japan sometimes, but I love it here. I think it's the most beautiful and one of the most exciting cities in the world.

Peter But do you find it stressful?

Akemi Not at all. I know Sydney is the biggest city in Australia, but remember, I'm from Tokyo.

Peter Oh, yeah. What else do you like about living here?

Akemi A lot of things. It's very clean and safe. The people are friendly. Oh, and the food here is fantastic.

Peter I agree. I think Sydney has the best restaurants in the country.

Akemi Hey, do you want to get something to eat?

Peter Sure. I know a nice café. It's cheap but good.

B **Listen to their conversation in the café. How does Akemi describe the café? How does Peter describe the food?**

3 Grammar Superlative adjectives

Sydney is **the biggest** city in Australia.
Sydney is one of **the most exciting** cities in the world.
Sydney has **the best** restaurants in the country.

What is **the cleanest** city in your country?
What city has **the most traditional** restaurants?
Is it the **worst** restaurant?
Yes, it is. No, it isn't.

Adjective	Superlative
clean	the cleanest
safe	the safest
big	the biggest
ugly	the ugliest
stressful	the most stressful
good	the best
bad	the worst

A Complete the questions with the superlative form of the adjectives. Then compare with a partner.

1 What's one of ______ (old) universities in your country?
2 What's ______ (big) city in your country?
3 What's ______ (modern) city in your country?
4 What's ______ (beautiful) national park?
5 What city has ______ (good) restaurants?
6 What city has ______ (bad) weather?

University of Cambridge

B Ask and answer the questions in Part A. Discuss your ideas.

4 Pronunciation Word stress

A Listen and repeat. Notice the stress in the names of these cities.

● •	• ●	● • •	• ● •
Sydney	Ma**drid**	**Can**berra	New **Del**hi

B Listen and write the cities in the correct columns in Part A. Then practice with a partner.

Amsterdam Berlin Caracas Lima

5 Speaking What's the . . .?

PAIR WORK **Ask and answer questions about your town or city.**

expensive / hotel	exciting / neighborhood	modern / building
beautiful / park	big / department store	relaxing / place

A: *What's the most expensive hotel?*
B: *I'm not sure it's the most expensive, but the Grand Hotel is very expensive.*

6 Keep talking!

Go to page 143 for more practice.

I can make comparisons about my city.

D The best place to go

1 Reading

A Read the message board. Who answers Miguel's question about safety?

Group posts

Topic: **Austin or San Antonio?**

7

miguel Posted May 17 7:06 p.m.
Hi! I live in Mexico and am planning to visit my uncle in Dallas, Texas, next year. I'd also like to visit Austin or San Antonio for a few days. I like the outdoors, local music, good food, friendly people, etc. Are both cities safe? Any other tips appreciated. Thanks! Miguel

rocker Posted May 17 7:23 p.m.
I'm a musician and I live in Austin. I think the music here is the best in Texas. In fact, Austin's nickname is "the Live Music Capital of the World." I can send you the names of some cool music clubs. We have fantastic restaurants here, too.

biker68 Posted May 17 8:54 p.m.
Definitely visit San Antonio. The River Walk is one of the most popular things for visitors to do. There's a lot to do outdoors here, too. And everyone in Texas is friendly. Check out my pics: **myphotos**

susanp Posted May 17 11:09 p.m.
I disagree with rocker. I think the music is better in San Antonio. I've lived in both cities. There is a lot to do outdoors in San Antonio, but there's just more to do in Austin.

richard Posted May 18 6:45 a.m.
Both cities are safe, by the way, so don't worry. I live in Houston. It's the largest city in Texas. You should visit here, too. ☺ Read my travel blog at richard23.cup.org.

traveler Posted May 18 10:31 a.m.
San Antonio has the best food in Texas. Do you like Tex-Mex food? You should go in spring or fall (summer is hot!). I suggest traveling by bus. It's not expensive. Email me with any questions.

miguel Posted May 18 3:22 p.m.
Miguel here again. Thanks, everyone!

B Read the message board again. Answer the questions. Check (✓) your answers.

Who . . .?	rocker	biker68	susanp	richard	traveler
lives in Houston	☐	☐	☐	☐	☐
gives a link to see pictures	☐	☐	☐	☐	☐
writes about the weather	☐	☐	☐	☐	☐
prefers the music in San Antonio	☐	☐	☐	☐	☐
has a travel blog	☐	☐	☐	☐	☐
is a musician	☐	☐	☐	☐	☐

C PAIR WORK What do you do when you need advice or a recommendation? Who do you talk to? Tell your partner.

2 Writing A message board

A Choose a topic for a message board. Then write a question asking for a recommendation about your topic. Use the model to help you.

- food
- music
- outdoor activities
- transportation

B GROUP WORK Pass your question to the classmate on your right. Read and answer your classmate's question. Continue to pass, read, and answer all the questions in your group.

C Read the answers to your question. Which recommendation is the best?

Can you suggest a good restaurant near our school?

1. You should go to Mickey's. It's fantastic, but it's expensive.
2. I think Thai Palace has the best food.
3. I agree. It's the most popular restaurant near here.

3 Speaking The best of the city

A PAIR WORK Complete the chart with information about the best things in your city or town. Give reasons.

The best things about ______	Reasons

A: I think the best thing about our city is the people. They are very friendly and helpful.
B: I agree.

B GROUP WORK Compare your ideas with another pair. Do you agree?

C CLASS ACTIVITY Make a list of all things from Parts A and B. Which is the most popular?

I can discuss aspects of a city.

Wrap-up

1 Quick pair review

Lesson A Brainstorm!

Make a list of fun places to see in a city. How many do you know? You have one minute.

Lesson B Do you remember?

Check (✓) the questions you can ask when you want a recommendation. You have one minute.

- ☐ What would you recommend doing there?
- ☐ Which place is more expensive?
- ☐ When are you going to China?
- ☐ What would you suggest doing there?
- ☐ What are you going to do in Brazil?
- ☐ What do you think I should do there?

Lesson C Test your partner!

Say an adjective to describe a city. Can your partner say the superlative? Take turns. You have one minute.

A: Modern.

B. The most modern.

Lesson D Guess!

Describe a city, but don't say its name. Can your partner guess what it is? Take turns. You and your partner have two minutes.

A: It's an old city in Europe. It's beautiful. It has a lot of squares and fountains.

B: Is it Florence?

A: Yes, it is.

2 In the real world

What city would you like to visit? Go to a travel website and find information about the city in English. Then write about it.

- What country is it in?
- What's it like?
- What is there to do in the city?
- What's it famous for?

Montreal

I would like to go to Montreal. It's in Canada. It's modern and safe . . .

9 People

LESSON A

- Careers
- *Was / were born*; past of *be*

LESSON B

- Expressing certainty
- Expressing uncertainty

LESSON C

- Personality adjectives
- Simple past; *ago*

LESSON D

- Reading: "A Different Kind of Banker"
- Writing: A biography

1

2

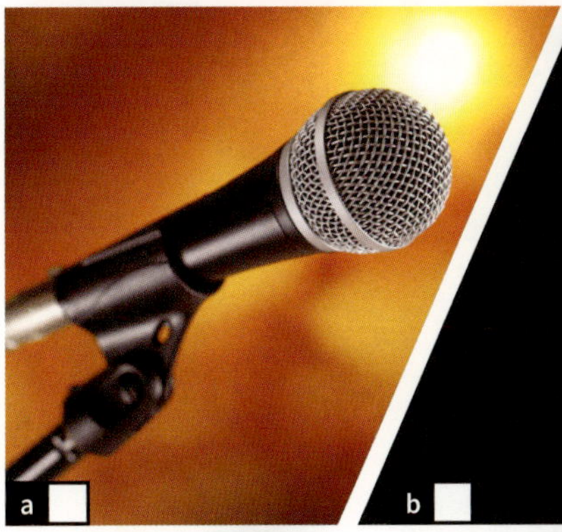
a

b

3

4

c

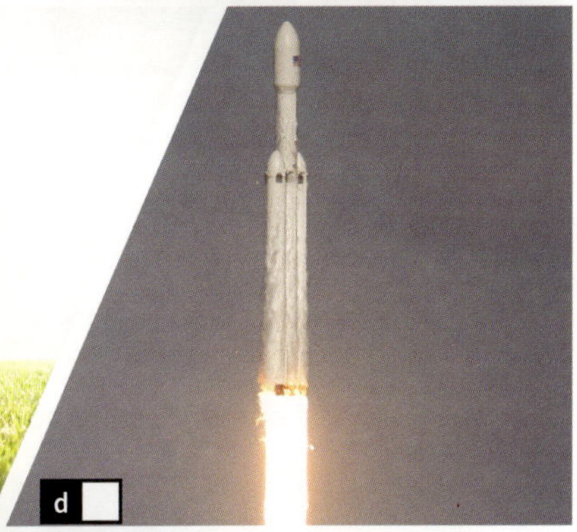
d

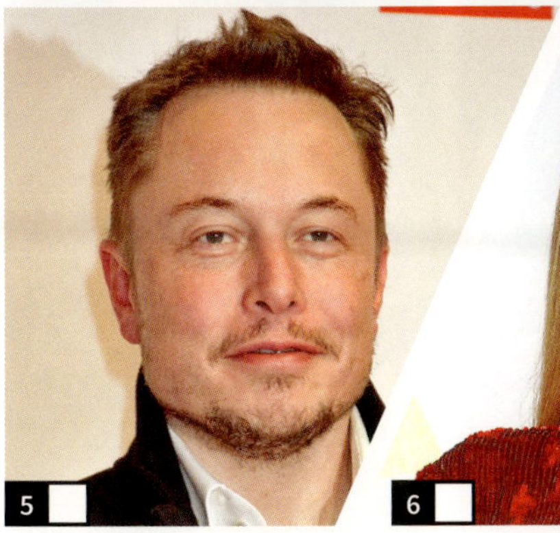
5

6

e

f

Warm-up

A Match the people and the things they are famous for. Check your answers on page 94.

B Which of the people in Part A would you like to meet? Why?

A Where was he born?

1 Vocabulary Careers

A Match the words and the pictures. Then listen and check your answers.

a	astronaut	c	composer	e	director	g	politician
b	athlete	d	designer	f	explorer	h	scientist

1 ☐ 
2 ☐ 
3 ☐ 

4 ☐ 
5 ☐ 
6 ☐ 
7 ☐ 
8 ☐ 

B PAIR WORK Give an example of a famous person for each category.

"Guillermo del Toro is a famous director."

2 Language in context Famous firsts

A Read about these famous firsts. Which famous first happened first?

Emilio Palma was born at Argentina's Esperanza Base in Antarctica in 1978. He was the first person born on the continent.

The first person on the moon in 1969 was American astronaut Neil Armstrong. He was on the moon for only two and a half hours.

Junko Tabei was the first woman to climb Mt. Everest in 1975. She was also the first woman to climb the highest mountains on all seven continents.

Venus and Serena Williams are great athletes. They were the first sisters to win Wimbledon in 2000.

B Which people from Part A would you like to meet? What question would you ask them?

3 Grammar *Was / were born; past of be*

Where **was** Emilio Palma **born**? He **was born** in Antarctica. He **wasn't born** in Argentina. Where **were** Venus and Serena **born**? They **were born** in the U.S. They **weren't born** in Canada. **Was** he **born** in Antarctica? Yes, he **was**. No, he **wasn't.**	How long **was** Neil Armstrong on the moon? He **was** there for two and a half hours. He **wasn't** there for very long. Where **were** his parents from? They **were** from Argentina. They **weren't** from Antarctica. **Were** they Wimbledon champions in 2000? Yes, they **were**. No, they **weren't**.

A Complete the sentences with the correct past form of *be*. Then compare with a partner.

1 Coco Chanel ________________ an amazing French designer.
2 Albert Einstein ________________ born in Germany.
3 Alfred Hitchcock ________________ a great director.
4 Diego Rivera and Frida Kahlo ________________ born in Mexico.
5 Mozart and Beethoven ________________ famous composers.

B Correct the false sentences. Then compare with a partner.

1 Ronald Reagan was a British politician. (American)
He wasn't a British politician. He was an American politician.
2 Zheng He was an early Chinese scientist. (explorer)
____
3 Artist Vincent van Gogh was born in the 20th century. (19th century)
____
4 Gianni Versace and Yves Saint Laurent were explorers. (designers)
____
5 Venus and Serena Williams were born in the late 1970s. (early 1980s)
____

4 Speaking *Famous people*

GROUP WORK Choose a person from the past. Your group asks questions and guesses the person's name. Take turns.

A: *He was from Mexico. He was a politician.*
B: *Is it . . . ?*
A: *No, sorry. He was born in the 19th century.*
C: *I think I know. Is it Benito Juárez?*

5 Keep talking!

Student A go to page 141 and Student B go to page 145 for more practice.

I can ask and talk about people from the past.

B I'm not sure, but I think . . .

1 Interactions Certainty and uncertainty

A **Look at the pictures. Where are the people? What are they doing?**

B **Listen to the conversation. Does Mike know the answer to both questions? Then practice the conversation.**

Mike Let's go over more questions before our test tomorrow.

Jenny OK. What was the original name of New York City?

Mike It was New Amsterdam.

Jenny Are you sure?

Mike I'm positive.

Jenny Correct! This one's more difficult. Who was Plato's teacher?

Mike I'm not sure, but I think it was Aristotle.

Jenny Actually, Aristotle was Plato's student. Socrates was his teacher.

Mike Oh, right.

C **Listen to the expressions. Then practice the conversation again with the new expressions.**

Expressing certainty		
I'm positive.	I'm certain.	I'm sure.

Expressing uncertainty		
I'm not sure, but I think . . .	I'm not certain, but I think . . .	I'm not positive, but I think . . .

D **Circle the answer you think is correct. Practice with a partner and use expressions from Part C. Then check your answers on page 94.**

1 Barack Obama was president of the **U.S.** / **U.K.**

2 Mozart was born in the **16th** / **17th** / **18th** century.

3 Neymar da Silva Santos, Jr's first soccer team was **Barcelona** / **Paris Saint-Germain** / **Santos**.

4 Che Guevara was born in **Bolivia** / **Argentina** / **Cuba**.

5 The 2016 Olympics were in **Sochi** / **Rio** / **Sydney**.

A: *Barack Obama was the president of the U.S.*

B: *Are you sure?*

A: *I'm positive.*

2 Listening Sorry, that's not right.

A Do you know the answers to these questions? Write your guesses in the first column.

		Your guess	Player's guess	
1	Where were the 2016 Olympics?			☐
2	Who was the winner of the 2014 World Cup?			☐
3	In what century was Pablo Picasso born?			☐
4	Who was the author of the play *Hamlet*?			☐
5	How long was Barack Obama president of the U.S.?			☐

B Listen to four friends play a board game. Write the players' guesses in the second column.

C Listen again. Check (✓) the players' guesses that are correct.

3 Speaking Do you know?

A PAIR WORK Look at the pictures and the categories. Add another category. Then write two questions for each category. Be sure you know the answers!

Actors and actresses

Athletes

Singers and musicians

B GROUP WORK Ask your questions. Use expressions of certainty or uncertainty in the answers.

A: *Where was Brad Pitt born?*

B: *I'm not sure, but I think he was born in . . .*

A: *How old is he?*

I can express certainty and uncertainty. ✓

C People I admire

1 Vocabulary Personality adjectives

A Match the words in the paragraphs and the definitions. Then listen and check your answers.

I admire U.S. President Abraham Lincoln. He was **honest**[1] as a lawyer and often worked for free. He was **brave**[2] and kept the country together during war. He was a very **inspiring**[3] person.

–Jin Ju

Nobel Prize in Literature winner Kazuo Ishiguro is very **passionate**[4] about his writing. He's very **intelligent**[5], and I really admire his novels.

–Celia

Bono is a **talented**[6] musician, but he's also a **caring**[7] person. I admire him for his fight against world poverty. He's very **determined**[8], and he's helping a lot of poor people.

–Mark

____ very good at something
_1_ open, telling the truth
____ not afraid of anything
____ nice to other people
____ making other people want to do something
____ able to understand things quickly and easily
____ trying everything possible to do something
____ showing a strong feeling about something

B PAIR WORK What other personality adjectives can you think of? Discuss your ideas.

2 Conversation I really admire him.

A Listen and practice.

Paul Did you finish your report, Emma?
Emma Yeah, I did. I finished it two days ago.
Paul Good for you! So who did you write about?
Emma Jacques Cousteau. I really admire him.
Paul I don't think I know him. What did he do?
Emma A lot! He was a French scientist and explorer. He loved nature and studied the sea. He made documentaries and wrote books about the world's oceans. He won a lot of prizes for his work.
Paul Wow! He sounds like an inspiring guy.
Emma He was. He was really passionate about his work.

B Listen to the rest of the conversation. When did Jacques Cousteau die?

3 Grammar Simple past; *ago*

Who **did** you **write** about? I **wrote** about Jacques Cousteau. I **didn't write** about his son. What **did** he **do**? He **made** documentaries. **Did** you **finish** your report? Yes, I **did**. No, I **didn't**.	**Period of time + *ago*** I finished the report **two days ago**. I researched it **a week ago**. I saw a documentary **four years ago**. He died **a long time ago**.

A Complete the conversation with the simple past form of the verbs. Then practice with a partner.

A Why ________ you ________ (decide) to write about Serena Williams for your report?

B Well, I ________ (want) to write about an athlete. And I think she's very inspiring. In 2008, she ________ (start) the Serena Williams Foundation. It builds schools. Then in 2010, she ________ (write) the book *My Life: Queen of the Court*.

A What else did she do?

B Well, in 2016, she ________ (dance) in her friend Beyoncé's video. In September 2017, she ________ (have) a baby girl!

B PAIR WORK **Ask and answer questions about when Serena Williams did these things. Use *ago* in the answers.**

have a baby	dance in a video	start a foundation	write a book

4 Pronunciation Simple past *-ed* endings

Listen and repeat. Notice the different ways the past simple endings are pronounced.

/t/		/d/		/id/	
finished	asked	played	admired	wanted	created

5 Speaking What did they do?

GROUP WORK **Use the adjectives to describe people you know. What did the people do?**

brave	caring	honest	intelligent	talented

"My sister Megumi is very brave. She traveled alone in Canada and . . ."

6 Keep Talking

Go to page 146 for more practice.

I can describe people I admire.

D Making a difference

1 Reading

A **Read the biography. How did Dr. Muhammad Yunus make a difference?**

a He won the Nobel Peace Prize. b He helped the poor. c He studied economics.

A DIFFERENT KIND OF BANKER

Dr. Muhammad Yunus, a banker and economist, was born in Bangladesh in 1940. He studied economics at Dhaka University in Bangladesh. He taught for a few years and then went to the United States to continue his studies. He returned home to Bangladesh in 1972 and started teaching again.

One day in 1976, Yunus visited a poor **village** in his home country. There he met some women who wanted to make furniture, but they didn't have enough money. He decided to help them and gave them $27 of his own money.

They made and sold the furniture, **made a profit**, and then returned the money to Dr. Yunus. At that point, he saw how very little money could help a lot. He decided to help poor people. A bank **loaned** him the money. In 1983, Yunus started Grameen Bank. This bank loans money to poor people. Dr. Yunus and Grameen Bank received the 2006 Nobel Peace Prize for their work with the poor.

In 2009, the bank had 7.95 million customers, and 97% of these customers were women. The success of the bank inspired other people in many different countries to start similar banks. Yunus once said, "**Conventional** banks look for the rich; we look for the absolutely poor."

B **Number these events from Dr. Yunus's life from 1 to 8.**

_____ He returned to Bangladesh.
_____ He was born in 1940.
_____ He started the Grameen Bank.
_____ He studied in the United States.
_____ He studied at Dhaka University.
_____ He gave money to some women in 1976.
_____ He won the Nobel Peace Prize.
_____ He inspired other people.

C **Read the biography again. Find the words in bold, and check (✓) the correct meaning.**

1 A **village** is:
☐ a very small town ☐ a big place where a lot of people live

2 If you **made a profit**, you:
☐ lost money ☐ made money

3 If someone **loaned** you money, you:
☐ gave back the money ☐ kept the money

4 A **conventional** bank is:
☐ usual ☐ unusual

D PAIR WORK **How would you describe Dr. Yunus? Tell your partner.**

2 Writing A biography

A PAIR WORK **Discuss famous people who made a big difference in people's lives. Answer the questions.**

- What are their names?
- What do you know about their lives?
- What did they do?
- How did they make a difference?

B **Write a short biography about a famous person who made a difference. Use the model and the answers in Part A to help you.**

José Antonio Abreu
José Antonio Abreu is a Venezuelan economist. He is also a talented musician. In 1975, he started a music school for poor children. He wanted to help these children and was determined to change their lives with music. Today, children all over Venezuela are playing in orchestras.

C GROUP WORK **Share your writing. Who do you think made the biggest difference?**

3 Listening Life lessons

A **Listen to three people describe the people who made a difference in their lives. Check (✓) the qualities they use to describe those people.**

	Qualities		What did the people teach them?
1	☐ caring ☐ talented	☐ intelligent ☐ creative	a. how to sing b. to be a musician
2	☐ brave ☐ honest	☐ generous ☐ determined	a. never to quit b. how to play soccer
3	☐ determined ☐ caring	☐ honest ☐ inspiring	a. how to teach English b. the qualities of a good teacher

B **Listen again. What did the people teach them? Circle the correct answers.**

4 Speaking In my life

GROUP WORK **Tell your group about a person who made a difference in your life. Use the questions below and your own ideas.**

- How do you know this person?
- What did he or she teach you?
- What did he or she do?
- How would you describe him or her?

A: My aunt made a difference in my life.

B: Oh, yeah? Why?

A: She taught me to think of other people.

I can describe people who made a difference. ✓

Wrap-up

1 Quick pair review

Lesson A Brainstorm!

Make a list of careers. How many do you know? You have two minutes.

Lesson B Guess!

Say the name of a famous person. Does your partner know where he or she was born? Take turns. You have two minutes.

A: Albert Einstein.
B: He was born in Germany.
A: Are you sure?
B: I'm positive.

B: Oprah Winfrey.
A: I'm not sure, but I think she was born in Mississippi.

Lesson C Test your partner!

Say six verbs. Can your partner write the simple past form of the verbs correctly? Check his or her answers. Take turns. You and your partner have two minutes.

1 ____________ 3 ____________ 5 ____________
2 ____________ 4 ____________ 6 ____________

Lesson D Find out!

Who are two people both you and your partner think made a difference in the world? What qualities do they have? Take turns. You and your partner have two minutes.

A: I think Nelson Mandela made a difference.
B: Me, too. He was determined and inspiring.
A: Yes, he was.

2 In the real world

Who do you admire? Go online and find five things that he or she did that you think are interesting. Then write about this person.

Sheryl Sandberg

I admire Sheryl Sandberg. She is the Chief Operating Officer of Facebook. She's a great businessperson. She also helps a lot of women and children . . .

Answers to Warm-up, Part A (page 85)
1. e 2. f 3. b 4. c 5. d 6. a

Answers to Interactions, Part D (page 88)
1. U.S. 2. 18th 3. Santos 4. Argentina 5. Rio

10 In a restaurant

LESSON A
- Menu items
- Articles

LESSON B
- Ordering food
- Checking information

LESSON C
- Interesting food
- Present perfect for experience

LESSON D
- Reading: "Restaurants with a Difference"
- Writing: A review

Warm Up

A What kinds of food do you think each place serves?

B Check (✓) the top three places you would like to try. Why?

A The ice cream is fantastic!

1 Vocabulary Menu items

A 🎧 **Label the menu with the correct words. Then listen and check your answers.**

Appetizers	Desserts	Main dishes	Side dishes

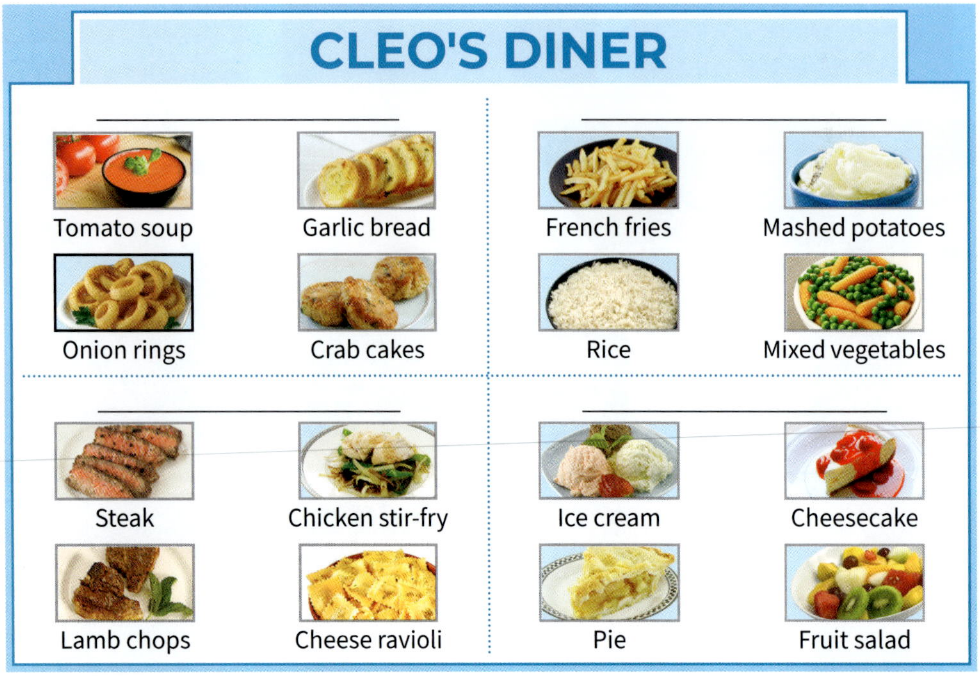

B PAIR WORK **Give an example of another menu item for each category.**

"Another example of a main dish is spaghetti with meatballs. Another side dish . . ."

2 Language in context Any recommendations?

A 🎧 **Listen to Jeff chat with his friends online. Who recommends the ice cream?**

Jeff I'm thinking of eating out tonight. Any recommendations?

Junko I'd recommend going to Cleo's Diner. They have great food and good service.

Tony12 Yeah, Cleo's is amazing. Get an appetizer there. They're excellent.

Jeff GR8! How are the main dishes?

Tony12 I had steak with some French fries. The steak was great, but the fries weren't.

Junko You should try a dessert there, too. The ice cream is fantastic!

Jeff I love ice cream! THX. 😉 Does anyone want to join me?

B **What about you? What do you do when you need a recommendation for a restaurant?**

3 Grammar Articles

Use a / an to talk about nonspecific singular count nouns	Use the to talk about specific count and noncount nouns.
Try **a** dessert.	I had **the** crab cakes.
Get **an** appetizer.	**The** ice cream is fantastic.
Use some *before plural count and noncount nouns.*	*Use* the *to name count and noncount nouns a second time.*
Let's order **some** French fries.	I had a steak and some French fries.
Let's order **some** garlic bread.	**The** steak was great, but **the** fries weren't.

Circle the words. Then compare with a partner.

A I'm glad we came here. It's a great place.
B So, do you want to share **an** / **some** appetizer?
A Sure. How about **an** / **the** onion rings?
B Perfect!
A And do you want to get **a** / **some** crab cakes?
B I don't think so. I'm not *that* hungry.
A I'm going to get **a** / **the** lamb chops with **a** / **some** rice.
B I think I want **a** / **the** steak. I heard it's delicious.
A **A** / **The** desserts are good. I love **an** / **the** ice cream.
B Yeah, we should order **a** / **an** dessert later.
A Let's find **the** / **some** waiter. Where is he?

4 Pronunciation *The* before vowel and consonant sounds

A Listen and repeat. Notice how *the* is pronounced before vowel and consonant sounds.

/i/		
the appetizer	the ice cream	the orange

/ə/		
the lamb	the fruit	the pie

B PAIR WORK Practice the conversation in Exercise 3.

5 Speaking What to order?

A PAIR WORK Do you usually order an appetizer, a main dish, a side dish, and a dessert in restaurants? Discuss your ideas.

A: I usually order a main dish and a side dish. I don't really like desserts.

B: I sometimes order an appetizer, but I always order a dessert.

B PAIR WORK Look at the menu in Exercise 1. What would you order?

"The chicken stir-fry and the rice look good. I'd order that."

6 Keep talking!

Go to page 147 for more practice.

I can talk about menus and eating out.

B I'll have the fish, please.

1 Interactions At a restaurant

A When was the last time you went to a restaurant? Who did you go with? What did you order?

B Listen to the conversation. What does Maria order? Then practice the conversation.

Waiter Are you ready to order?
Maria Yes, I think so.
Waiter What would you like?
Maria I'll have the fish with some rice, and a small salad, please.
Waiter Anything else?
Maria No, I don't think so.
Waiter All right. Let me check that. You'd like the fish, with rice, and a small salad.
Maria Yes, that's right.
Waiter Would you like some water?
Maria Sure, that would be great. Thank you.

C Listen to the expressions. Then practice the conversation again with the new expressions.

Ordering food

I'll have . . ., please. | I'd like . . ., please. | Can I have . . .,please?

Checking information

Let me check that. | Let me read that back. | Let me repeat that.

D PAIR WORK Have conversations like the one in Part B. Use the food below.

2 Listening Food orders

A Listen to people order food. How many people order dessert? Circle the correct answer.

one two three

B Listen again. Correct any wrong information on these orders.

1

Mickey's

chicken
rice
mixed vegetables
apple pie

2

Mickey's

crab cakes
lamb chops
French fries
small salad
water
chocolate cake
medium mushroom pizza
iced tea

3 Speaking Role play

PAIR WORK **Role-play the situation. Then change roles.**

Student A: You are waiter or waitress at Puck's Place. Greet the customer, take his or her order, and then check the information.

Student B: You are a customer at Puck's Place. Order from the menu.

PUCK'S PLACE

PUCK'S PLACE

Appetizers
Chicken salad • Pasta salad • Onion soup
Chicken soup • Crab cakes • Garlic bread

Main dishes
Lamb chops • Steak
Chicken stir-fry • Fish • Cheese ravioli

Sides
French fries • Rice
Mixed vegetables • Mashed potatoes

Desserts
Apple pie • Chocolate ice cream • Fruit salad

Drinks
Tea • Coffee • Lemonade • Soda

A: Hello. Are you ready to order?

B: Yes. I'll have the onion soup. And can I have the fish and some white rice, please? Also, . . .

I can order food in a restaurant.

C Have you ever . . .?

1 Vocabulary Interesting food

A Complete the chart with the correct words. Then listen and check your answers.

avocados

blue cheese

carrot juice

dates

frozen yogurt

oysters

plantains

seaweed

soy milk

squid

Dairy	Seafood	Fruits / Vegetables	Drinks

B PAIR WORK **Which food in Part A do you like? do you dislike? would you like to try? Tell your partner.**

"I like oysters. I don't like carrot juice. I'd like to try squid."

2 Conversation Dinner plans

A Listen and practice.

Ellen What are you doing tonight?

Peter I'm going to World Café with my brother. Have you ever been there?

Ellen No, I haven't. But I heard it's good.

Peter I looked at their menu online this morning. They serve some really interesting food.

Ellen Oh, yeah? Like what?

Peter Fresh oysters. I've never had oysters, so I want to try them. Have you ever eaten them?

Ellen Yeah, I have. I think they're delicious.

Peter I've had squid. Are they similar?

Ellen Um, not really. Do they only serve seafood?

Peter No, they serve a little of everything.

B Listen to Peter's message to Ellen the next day. What food did he like?

3 Grammar Present perfect for experience

I've **been** to World Café.	I **haven't tried** the desserts.
I've **had** squid.	I've never **eaten** oysters.
Have you **ever been** to World Café?	
Yes, I **have**. No, I **haven't**.	
Contractions I've = I have	I haven't = I have not.

Past participles	
be	**been**
drink	**drunk**
eat	**eaten**
have	**had**
try	**tried**

A Complete the conversations with the present perfect form of the verbs. Then practice with a partner.

1 A This place looks fun. I ________________ (never / be) here.
B I love it here. I ________________ (be) here many times.
A Everything looks delicious.
B ________ you ________ (ever / eat) Mexican food before?
A I ________________ (have) tacos, but I'd like to try something new.

2 A I ________________ (never / try) frozen yogurt. Can you recommend a flavor?
B I ________________ (have) most flavors, and they're all good.
A ________ you ________ (ever / try) the green tea flavor?
B No, I ________________ (have / not), but you should try it!

B Make sentences about your food experiences.

1 be / to a Turkish restaurant ________________
2 eat / oysters ________________
3 drink / soy milk ________________
4 have / plantains ________________
5 try / blue cheese ________________

C PAIR WORK Ask *Have you ever . . .?* questions about the experiences in Part B.

4 Speaking Food experiences

A Add two more food experiences to the list.

eat / dates	have / seaweed	________ / ________
try / Vietnamese food	drink / carrot juice	________ / ________

B PAIR WORK Discuss your experiences. What food would you like to try?

A: *Have you ever tried Vietnamese food?*

B: *Yes, I have. It's delicious.*

5 Keep talking!

Go to page 148 for more practice.

I can ask about and describe food experiences.

D Restaurant experiences

1 Reading

A Read the web page. Which sentence describes all three restaurants? Check (✓) the correct answer.

- ☐ They don't have a lot of light.
- ☐ They're not very expensive.
- ☐ They are in good locations.
- ☐ They are very unusual.

RESTAURANTS WITH A DIFFERENCE

Ninja Akasaka is a popular restaurant in Tokyo. A ninja in dark clothes greets guests at the door and takes them through the dark hallways of the ninja house to their tables. The waiters also dress as ninjas. Ninja Akasaka has over a hundred delicious dishes to choose from. There's also a branch of the restaurant in Manhattan – Ninja New York.

95 likes Follow

Annalakshmi is a vegetarian restaurant in Chennai, India, with additional restaurants in three other countries. There are no prices on the menu, so guests pay what they can! The people who work there are volunteers and take turns serving customers, cleaning tables, and washing dishes. Indian art covers the walls, and there are even live music and dance performances.

78 likes Follow

At ***Dans Le Noir*** (In the Dark) in Paris, guests order their food in a place with a lot of light, but then they eat in darkness. They focus on the touch, smell, and taste of the food. The waiters there are blind, so when guests are ready to leave, they call the waiter's name. Their waiter then takes them back to the place where they ordered the food. There are additional restaurants in London and Moscow.

64 likes Follow

B Read the web page again. Write T (true), F (false), or NI (no information) next to the sentences.

1. Guests dress as ninjas at Ninja Akasaka. ______
2. Ninja New York is more popular than Ninja Akasaka. ______
3. Annalakshmi has restaurants in four countries. ______
4. Every guest at Annalakshmi pays the same price. ______
5. Guests never see their food at Dans Le Noir. ______
6. The cooks at Dans Le Noir are blind. ______

C PAIR WORK Which restaurants in Part A do you think you'd enjoy? Why? Have you ever been to an unusual restaurant? Tell your partner.

2 Listening So, what did you think?

A 🎧 **Listen to three couples talk about the restaurants in Exercise 1. Where did each couple eat? Number the restaurants from 1 to 3.**

☐ Ninja Akasaka ☐ Annalakshmi ☐ Dans Le Noir

B 🎧 **Listen again. Check (✓) the things each couple liked about the experience.**

	the service	the prices	the location	the food
1	☐	☐	☐	☐
2	☐	☐	☐	☐
3	☐	☐	☐	☐

3 Writing A review

A Think of a restaurant you like. Answer the questions.

- What is the name of the restaurant?
- What type of food does it serve?
- When were you there last?
- What would you recommend ordering?
- What do you like about the restaurant?

B Write a short review of your favorite restaurant. Use the model and your answers from Part A to help you.

My Favorite Restaurant
Seoul Barbecue is my favorite restaurant. It serves delicious, healthy Korean food. I went there last week and loved it. I ordered beef, and I had some small side dishes. I would recommend doing that. It's fun because you cook your own meat at the table. It's a little expensive, but I really liked the service. I'd recommend this restaurant.

C CLASS ACTIVITY **Post your reviews around the room. Read your classmates' reviews. Then get more information about the restaurant that interests you the most.**

4 Speaking Restaurant recommendations

PAIR WORK **Recommend a good place to go for each situation. Discuss your ideas.**

- take an overseas visitor
- meet a big group of friends
- have a child's birthday party
- have a quiet dinner for two
- get a quick, cheap lunch
- enjoy live music

A: What's a good place to meet a big group of friends?
B: How about . . .? There's a private room for big groups.

I can describe restaurant experiences. ✓

Wrap-up

1 Quick pair review

Lesson A Brainstorm!

Make a list of menu items. How many do you know? You have two minutes.

Lesson B Do you remember?

Check (✓) the things you can say to order food. You have one minute.

- ☐ I'll have some French fries, please.
- ☐ Try the cheesecake, please.
- ☐ What would you like?
- ☐ Can I have the steak, please?
- ☐ Let me check that.
- ☐ I'd like some pie, please.

Lesson C Find out!

What interesting food have you and your partner both tried? Take turns. You and your partner have two minutes.

A: *I've eaten squid.*

B: *I haven't. I've eaten . . .*

Lesson D Guess!

Describe a restaurant in your city, but don't say its name. Can your partner guess which one it is? Take turns. You and your partner have two minutes.

A: *This restaurant is on Main Street. It has good seafood, and the food is cheap. The service is fantastic.*

B: *Is it Big Fish?*

A: *Yes, it is.*

2 In the real world

What would you like to order? Go online and find a menu for a restaurant in English. Then write about it.

- What is the name of the restaurant?
- What appetizers, main dish, and side dishes would you like to order?
- What drink would you like to try?
- What dessert would you like to eat?

Alphabet Café
I'd like to eat at Alphabet Café. I'd like some garlic bread and the spaghetti . . .

11 Entertainment

LESSON A

- Types of movies
- *So, too, either,* and *neither*

LESSON B

- Asking for suggestions
- Giving a suggestion

LESSON C

- Types of music
- Determiners

LESSON D

- Reading: "Everybody Loves a Sing-Off"
- Writing: A popular musician

a

b

c

d

e

f

Warm Up

A Match the words and the pictures.

_______ an amusement park	_______ a dance performance	_______ a play
_______ a concert	_______ a movie	_______ a soccer game

B Which of these types of entertainment do you want to go to? Rank them from 1 (really want to go) to 6 (don't really want to go).

A I'm not a fan of dramas.

1 Vocabulary Types of movies

A Match the types of movies and the pictures. Then listen and check your answers.

a an action movie	c a comedy	e a horror movie	g a science fiction movie
b an animated movie	d a drama	f a musical	h a western

1 

2 

3 

4 

5 

6 

7 

8 

B PAIR WORK What are your favorite types of movies? Give an example of the types you like. Tell your partner.

"I love action movies and dramas. My favorite movies are . . ."

2 Language in context At the movies

A Listen to two friends at the movies. What type of movie are they watching?

B What about you? Are you ever late for movies? Do you like to sit in the front, middle, or back?

3 Grammar *So, too, either,* and *neither*

I'm a fan of science fiction movies. **So** am I / I am, **too**. Oh, I'm not. I like comedies. I like to sit in the front row. **So** do I. / I do, **too**. Really? I don't. I prefer the back row.	I'm not usually late for movies. **Neither** am I. / I'm not, **either**. Oh, I am. I'm always late. I don't buy popcorn. **Neither** do I. / I don't, **either**. Oh, I do. And I always get a soda.

A **Respond to the sentences in two different ways. Use *so*, *too*, *either*, or *neither*. Compare with a partner.**

1 I'm not a fan of dramas. Neither am I. / I'm not, either.
2 I love animated movies. ______ ______
3 I'm not interested in action movies. ______ ______
4 I'm interested in old westerns. ______ ______
5 I don't watch horror movies. ______ ______
6 I don't like science fiction movies. ______ ______

B PAIR WORK **Make the sentences in Part A true for you. Respond with *so*, *too*, *either*, or *neither*.**

A: I'm not a fan of dramas.
B: Neither am I. **OR** Really? I am. My favorite drama is . . .

4 Speaking Movie talk

A **Complete the sentences with true information.**

I like to eat ______candy______ at the movies.
(snack)

I really like ______________________.
(actor or actress)

I'm not a fan of ______________________.
(actor or actress)

I want to see ______________________.
(name of movie)

I don't really want to see ______________________.
(name of movie)

I often see movies at ______________________.
(name of theater)

I usually see movies with ______________________.
(name of person)

B PAIR WORK **Take turns reading your sentences. Respond appropriately.**

A: I like to eat candy at the movies.
B: I don't. I like to eat popcorn.

C GROUP WORK **What movies are playing right now? Which ones do you want to see? Can you agree on a movie to see together?**

5 Keep talking!

Go to page 149 for more practice.

I can talk about my movie habits and opinions.

B Any suggestions?

1 Interactions Suggestions

A What do you like to do on weekends? Who do you usually spend weekends with? How do you decide what to do?

B Listen to the conversation. What do they decide to do on the weekend? Then practice the conversation.

Douglas What do you want to do this weekend?

Jocelyn I don't really know. Do you have any suggestions?

Douglas Well, there's an outdoor movie in the park, a food festival, and a karaoke contest.

Jocelyn I hate karaoke, and we went to the movies last week.

Douglas Let's go to the food festival.

Jocelyn OK. That sounds good. Have you ever been to one?

Douglas No, but it sounds like a lot of fun.

C Listen to the expressions. Then practice the conversation again with the new expressions.

Asking for suggestions

- Do you have any suggestions?
- What do you suggest?
- Any suggestions?

Giving a suggestion

- Let's . . .
- Why don't we . . .?
- We could . . .

D Number the sentences from 1 to 8. Then practice with a partner.

____ A A play? That's not a bad idea.

____ A I'm not sure. We could see a movie.

__1__ A Let's do something different tonight.

____ A Why don't we see the comedy?

____ B We always see movies. Why don't we see a play?

____ B OK. And let's have dinner before.

____ B There are two plays. One is a drama, the other a comedy.

__2__ B OK. What do you suggest?

2 Listening Let's get together!

A Listen to three conversations. Check (✓) what the people decide to do.

	What they decide to do		Place	Time
1	☐ go to a movie	☐ watch a movie at home		
2	☐ go out to eat	☐ order take-out food		
3	☐ go to a play	☐ go to a baseball game		

B Listen again. Where and when are they going to meet? Write the place and time.

3 Speaking This weekend

A PAIR WORK Complete the chart with what is happening this weekend where you live.

	Movies	Music	Sports	Festivals
Friday				
Saturday				
Sunday				

B PAIR WORK Work with a new partner. Look at your charts. Decide to do three things together.

A: *Let's do something fun this weekend.*

B: *All right. Any suggestions?*

A: *Well, we could see the new horror movie. Do you like horror movies?*

B: *No, I don't. Sorry. Why don't we . . . ?*

I can ask for and give suggestions.

C All of us love music.

1 Vocabulary Types of music

A 🎧 **Listen to the song clips. Number the types of music you hear from 1 to 10. Then check your answers.**

pop

rock

jazz

country

classical

folk

hip-hop

techno

reggae

blues

B PAIR WORK **Say the name of a musician for each type of music in Part A. Tell your partner.**

"Jennifer Lopez sings pop music."

2 Conversation A music recital

A 🎧 **Listen and practice.**

Ingrid These kids are great musicians. Do all of the students at this school learn a musical instrument?

John No, I don't think so, but most of them do.

Ingrid I see. And do most of the schools in this city have bands?

John I'm not sure. I know a lot of them around here do. Some of the schools even have their own jazz bands.

Ingrid How interesting! Do you know what's next?

John I think there's going to be a violin solo.

B 🎧 **Listen to their conversation after the recital. What type of music do the children prefer to play?**

3 Grammar Determiners

100% → 0%		
100%	All of	
	Most of	
	A lot of	
	Some of	the students learn a **musical instrument.**
	Not many of	
0%	None of	

A Look at the picture of the Branson family. Complete the sentences with determiners. Then compare with a partner.

1 ________ of them are singing.
2 ________ of them have costumes.
3 ________ of them are sitting.
4 ________ of them are playing an instrument.
5 ________ of them have blond hair.
6 ________ of them are dancing.

B Make true sentences using determiners. Tell your partner.

1 . . . of my favorite songs are pop songs.
2 . . . of my friends play an instrument.
3 . . . of my classmates play in rock bands.
4 . . . of my friends enjoy singing karaoke.

4 Pronunciation Reduction of *of*

A Listen and repeat. Notice how *of* is sometimes pronounced /ə/ before consonant sounds.

/ə/	/ə/	/ə/
All of the students	A lot of the schools	None of my friends

B PAIR WORK Practice the sentences in Exercise 3A. Reduce *of* to /ə/.

5 Speaking Ask the class.

**A CLASS ACTIVITY Add a type of music, a song, or a singer to the question.
Then ask your classmates the question.
Write the number of people who answer "yes."**

Do you like ________________ ? ☐

B Share your information. Use determiners.

"Some of us like hip-hop."

6 Keep talking!

Go to page 150 for more practice.

I can report the results of a survey.

D Singing shows around the world

1 Reading

A Read the online article. Which people are most interested in famous singers?

EVERYBODY LOVES A SING-OFF

Every year, thousands of people around the world enter singing competitions on TV, and millions of people watch to see who wins. Why do we love these programs so much?

Kanda, Thailand
Favorite show: The Mask Singer
"I'm a fan because I like seeing regular people become famous. Everybody loves a rags-to-riches story, right? I really enjoy shows where you choose favorites and watch them improve each week. Also, I love when I can vote for a singer – it's fun to help decide who will be the next big star!"

Andrew, USA
Favorite show: American Idol
"I usually watch singing competitions because I want to see singers before they are stars. Did you know that singers like Justin Timberlake, Beyoncé, and One Direction were all on TV competitions? Not many of the competitors will become famous – but sometimes, I hear a singer and I just know she's going to be great."

Eduardo, Chile
Favorite show: Festival Internacional de la Canción de Viña del Mar
"Everybody likes to sing – that's why these competitions are so popular. All of my friends sing in the shower, in the car, walking down the street. But I wish it wasn't all pop music. How about a hip-hop competition? Or a techno contest with DJs? That would be really cool."

Wiktoria, Poland
Favorite show: Eurovision
"I like to watch people sing badly. Seriously, I can hear good singing any time on the radio — it's more fun to hear people who aren't so good. I like to see what happens when people get on stage with a big audience. Will they perform well? Or will they miss a beat? That's really why most of us watch – we like to be the judge."

B Read the article again. Answer the questions.

1 Why does Kanda watch singing shows? ______

2 What does Andrew want to see? ______

3 What does Yandri not like about competitions? ______

4 Why does Wiktoria like to see people sing badly? ______

C GROUP WORK **Do you like to watch singing competitions? Why or why not? Would you enter a competition? What kind of music would you sing? Discuss your ideas.**

2 Listening Classical music hour

A Listen to a radio host talk about the musician Lang Lang. Where is Lang Lang from?

B Listen again. Check (✓) the correct answers.

1 1. Lang Lang had his first music lessons at age:
- ☐ three ☐ five

2 He received his first award at age:
- ☐ five ☐ fifteen

3 He likes to share music with:
- ☐ young people ☐ older people

4 He also works with:
- ☐ UNICEF ☐ United Nations University

5 Besides classical music he loves:
- ☐ jazz and rock ☐ jazz, hip-hop, and pop

3 Writing A popular musician

A Think of your favorite musician or a popular musician. Answer the questions.

- Where is this person from?
- What type of music is this person famous for?
- What is this person's best song?
- What is interesting about this person?

B Write a short description about the musician. Use the model and your answers from Part A to help you.

My Favorite Singer

My favorite singer is Thalia. She's from Mexico. She sings different types of music, but mostly she sings pop and dance music. My favorite song is "No, No, No." She records songs in many languages. She sings in English, Spanish, French, and Tagalog.

C GROUP WORK Share your writing. Did any of you write about the same musician?

4 Speaking Make a playlist

A PAIR WORK Make a list of the most important singers, bands, or musicians from your country. What are their most popular songs?

B PAIR WORK Create a five-track playlist. Use your notes.

A: I think . . . is very important.

B: So do I. A lot of young people like his music.

C GROUP WORK Present your playlist and explain your choices. Ask and answer questions to get more information.

I can describe important singers and musicians.

Wrap-up

1 Quick pair review

Lesson A Find out!

What are two types of movies that both you and your partner like? You have two minutes.

A: *I like action movies. Do you?*

B: *No, but I like animated movies. Do you?*

Lesson B Do you remember?

Match the questions with the suggestions. You have one minute.

1 We should see a movie. Do you have any suggestions? ______
2 I'm hungry. Any suggestions? ______
3 Let's get some exercise. What do you suggest? ______
4 Where should we go shopping? Any suggestions? ______
5 We need to take a vacation? What do you suggest? ______

a We could take a walk.
b Why don't we go to the market?
c We could see a comedy.
d Why don't we go to Mexico?
e Let's make pizza!

Lesson C Brainstorm!

Make a list of types of music. How many do you know? Take turns. You and your partner have two minutes.

Lesson D Guess!

Describe a popular band or singer, but don't say the name. Can your partner guess the name? Take turns. You and your partner have two minutes.

A: *She sings pop music. She sings in Korean and Japanese. She's also an actress.*

B: *BoA?*

A: *Yes. Her real name is Kwon Bo-ah.*

2 In the real world

What were some of the top movies this year? Go online and find information about one of them in English. Then write about it.

- What's the name of the movie?
- What actors are in it?
- What type of movie is it?
- What songs are in the movie?

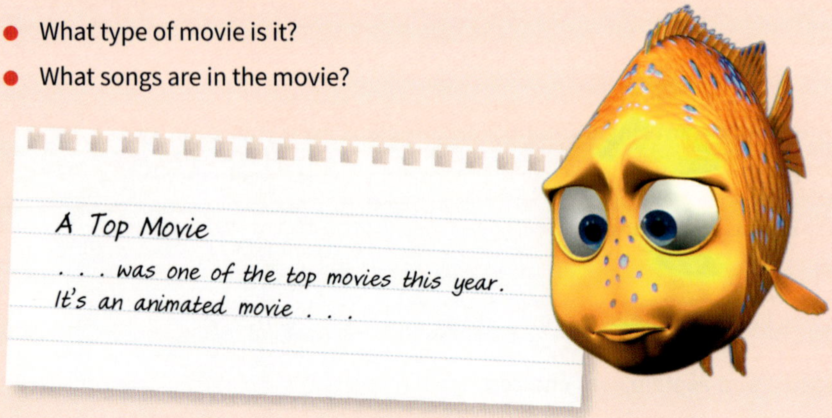

12 Time for a change

LESSON A

- Personal goals
- Infinitives of purpose

LESSON B

- Reacting to bad news
- Reacting to good news

LESSON C

- Milestones
- *Will* for predictions; *may*, *might* for possibility

LESSON D

- Reading: "An Olympic Dream Flies High"
- Writing: A dream come true

Warm-up

A The people in the pictures have made changes in their lives. What change do you think each person made?

B Would you like to make any of these changes? Which ones?

A Personal change

1 Vocabulary Personal goals

A Match the words and the pictures. Then listen and check your answers.

a get a credit card	**d** lose weight	**g** save money
b join a gym	**e** make more friends	**h** start a new hobby
c learn an instrument	**f** pass a test	**i** work / study harder

1 

2 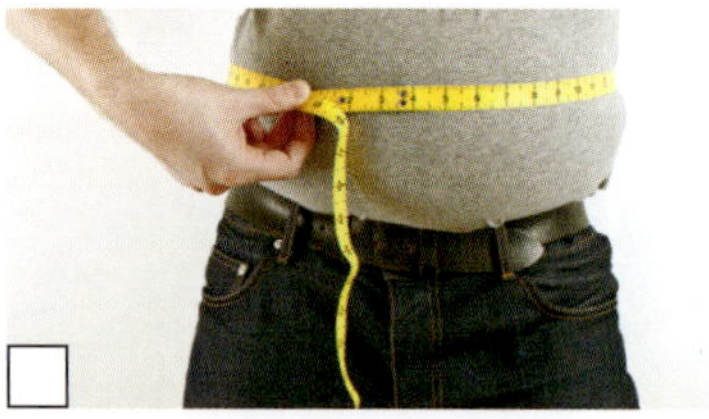

3 

4 

5 

6 

7 

8 

9 

B PAIR WORK **Which things in Part A are easy to do? Which are more difficult? Why? Tell your partner.**

"It's difficult to learn an instrument. It takes a long time!"

2 Language in context I'm making it happen!

A Listen to three people talk about changes. Who's learning something new?

My friends and I are starting our own band next year. I can sing, but I can't play an instrument, so I'm taking a class to learn the guitar.

–Leonardo

I joined a gym last month to lose weight. I only want to lose a couple of kilos, but I'm finding it difficult. But I'm making some new friends, so that's good.

–Mark

I hated taking the bus to work, so I saved money to buy a bike. Now I ride it to work every day, and I feel a lot healthier and happier.

–Tina

B Talk about a change you made.

3 Grammar Infinitives of purpose

I'm taking a class **to learn** the guitar.	(= because I want to learn the guitar)
I joined a gym last month **to lose** weight.	(= because I want to lose weight)
She'd like to save money **to buy** a bike.	(= because she wants to buy a bike)
We're starting a book club in July **to make** more friends.	(= because we want to make more friends)

A Match the sentence parts. Then compare with a partner.

1	I joined a gym last week	to buy a car.
2	I'm saving my money	to get better grades.
3	I'd like to go to the U.S.	to relax.
4	I studied harder	to improve my English.
5	I listen to music	to lose weight.

B Rewrite these sentences. Use an infinitive of purpose. Then compare with a partner.

1 I'd like to go to a hair salon because I want to get a new hairstyle.
I'd like to go to a hair salon to get a new hairstyle.

2 I listen to songs in English because I want to improve my listening.

3 I saved my money because I wanted to buy a new computer.

4 I'm studying on weekends because I want to get a better job.

C PAIR WORK Which sentences from Part B are true for you? Tell your partner.

4 Speaking Three changes

A Complete the chart with three changes you would like to make. Then think about the reasons why you would like to make each change.

	Changes	Reasons
1		
2		
3		

B GROUP WORK Discuss your changes. Are any of your changes or reasons the same?

"I'd like to go to Canada to study English. I hope to be an English teacher someday."

5 Keep talking!

Go to page 151 for more practice.

I can give reasons for personal changes.

B I'm happy to hear that!

1 Interactions Good and bad news

A Do you ever see old classmates or friends around town? What kinds of things do you talk about?

B Listen to the conversation. What's changed for Emily? Then practice the conversation.

Joe Hey, Emily. Long time no see.

Emily Oh, hi, Joe. How are you doing?

Joe Fine. Well, actually, I didn't pass my driving test – again. That's three times now.

Emily **That's too bad.**

Joe Yeah, I wanted to drive to the beach this weekend. So, what's new with you?

Emily Well, I'm playing guitar in a band. I'm really enjoying it.

Joe **That's wonderful!** What kind of music?

Emily Rock. We have a show next week. Do you want to come? I'll email you the information.

Joe Thanks. I'll be there!

C Listen to the expressions. Then practice the conversation again with the new expressions.

Reacting to bad news

- That's too bad.
- That's a shame.
- I'm sorry to hear that.

Reacting to good news

- That's wonderful!
- That's great to hear!
- I'm happy to hear that!

D PAIR WORK **Share the news below and react appropriately.**

I'm learning German.
I bought a car.
I failed my math exam.
I have a part-time job.
I broke my foot.
I lost my wallet.
I won two concert tickets.
I'm going to travel to London.
I'm not sleeping well.
I'm planning to get a pet.

2 Listening Sharing news

A Look at the pictures in Part B. Where are the people?

B Listen to four people share news with friends. What news are they talking about? Number the pictures from 1 to 4.

C Listen again. Correct the false sentences. Then compare with a partner.

1 Mark has some free time in the afternoons and evenings.
2 Lucia is saving her money to buy a restaurant.
3 Jeff is taking the train because his new car isn't running very well.
4 Wendy and her cousin had a terrible time in Rome and Florence.

3 Speaking Good news, bad news

A Complete the chart with some good news and bad news. (Don't use true news!)

	Good news		Bad news
1		1	
2		2	

B Class activity Share your news. React appropriately.

A: Hi, Mariko. What's new with you?
B: Well, I'm going to Paris next week to study French.
A: That's wonderful!
B: What's new with you?

C GROUP WORK Share the most interesting news you heard.

I can react to good and bad news.

C I think I'll get a job.

1 Vocabulary Milestones

A Complete the chart with the correct milestones. Then listen and check your answers.

☐ buy a house

☐ get promoted

☐ go to college

☐ graduate from high school

☐ rent an apartment

☐ retire

☐ start a career

☐ get married

☐ start school

Personal milestones	Educational milestones	Work-related milestones

B Number the milestones from 1 to 9 in the order that they usually happen. Then compare with a partner.

2 Conversation I'll go traveling.

A Listen and practice.

Tim Hey, Craig. How are you doing?

Craig Oh, hi, Tim. I'm fine. What's new with you?

Tim Well, I'm graduating from college this summer.

Craig That's wonderful! What do you think you'll do in September?

Tim I think I'll go traveling with some friends.

Craig That sounds fun, but it won't be cheap.

Tim Yeah, so I may get a job this summer to pay for the trip.

B Listen to the rest of the conversation. What's new with Craig?

3 Grammar Will for predictions; may, might for possibility

What do you think you'll do?	
Predictions I think **I'll go** traveling with some friends. I **won't get** a roommate. Do you think you**'ll get** a roommate? Yes, I**'ll get** one soon. No. I **won't get** a roommate this year.	*Possibility* I don't really know. I **may get** a job. I'm not really sure. I **might buy** a pet.

A Circle the correct words. Then practice with a partner.

1 A Do you think you'll buy a house next year?
  B No. I don't have enough money. But **I'll / I may** rent an apartment. I don't know.
2 A What do you think you'll do on your next birthday?
  B **I'll / I might** have a big party, but I'm not sure.
3 A When do you think you'll retire?
  B **I'll / I may** retire at 65. Most other people do.
4 A Do you think you'll buy a car this year?
  B No, **I won't / I might**. I don't have enough money for one.
5 A Do you think you'll get married after college?
  B I'm not sure. **I'll / I may** get married someday.

B PAIR WORK **Ask and answer the questions in Part A. Answer with your own information.**

4 Pronunciation Contraction of *will*

Listen and repeat. Notice how these pronouns + *will* are contracted into one syllable.

I'll you'll he'll she'll we'll they'll

5 Speaking My future

A Write an idea for each of the things below.

1 an important thing to do: ______________
2 an exciting thing to do: ______________
3 an expensive thing to buy: ______________
4 an interesting person to meet: ______________

B PAIR WORK **Ask and answer questions about the things in Part A. Use *will*, *may*, or *might* and these time expressions.**

A: *Do you think you'll start your career this year?*
B: *Yes, I think I will. I have an interview this week.*

Time expressions	
this week	this month
this weekend	next month
next week	this year

6 Keep talking!

Go to page 152 for more practice.

I can make predictions about the future.

D Dreams and aspirations

1 Reading

A Look at this quote. What do you think it means?

"The important thing in life is not to win but to try."

–Pierre de Coubertin, founder of the modern Olympic games

B Read the article. Check (✓) the best title.

- ☐ Skater Loses Olympics but Wins Fans
- ☐ The Worst Olympian Ever
- ☐ An Olympic Dream Flies High
- ☐ Ski Jumper – or Ski Dropper?

At the 1988 Winter Olympics, the most famous competitor wasn't the fastest skier or the strongest ice skater. He didn't win a gold medal – or any medals at all. In fact, Eddie Edwards finished last in the ski jumping competition. But his courage made him a favorite of fans around the world, who nicknamed him "Eddie the Eagle."

Eddie was a construction worker from a small town in England. He had a dream to make the Olympic team. He was a good skier and almost made the British team in 1984. For the 1988 games, he became England's #1 ski jumper for a simple reason – nobody else wanted to try.

Eddie had no money and no coach. He saved money to buy used equipment – his ski boots were too big, so he wore six pairs of socks. He didn't see very well and wore thick glasses. "Sometimes I take off, and I can't see where I'm going," he said. Before each jump, he was afraid that he might fall. But he worked hard to learn and to improve.

At the Olympic Games in Calgary, Eddie competed in the 70m and 90m jumps. He landed without falling, but came in last in both events.

Many people loved Eddie for his dream and his courage. But others thought he wasn't good enough to compete. To these people, Eddie said, "Where is it written that the Olympics are only for winners?"

Eddie's performance made him famous in England. When he returned home, 10,000 people met him at the airport. Today, Eddie is a construction worker again, but he is also famous thanks to the 2016 film, "Eddie the Eagle."

C Read the article again. Answer the questions.

1. What was Eddie's dream? ______
2. What was Eddie afraid of? ______
3. Why did the crowd like Eddie? ______
4. Why did many people like Eddie? ______

D GROUP WORK Do you think it's more important to win or to try? Should the Olympic Games be open to athletes like Eddie, or only the best athletes?

2 Listening An interview with an athlete

A 🎧 **Listen to an interview with Suzanne, a marathon runner. Check (✓) the two dreams she's achieved.**

- ☐ to run marathons
- ☐ to go back to school
- ☐ to win the Chicago Marathon
- ☐ to run all the big marathons

B 🎧 **Listen again. Circle the correct answers.**

1. This is Suzanne's **fifth** / **seventh** marathon.
2. She **won** / **didn't win** the Boston Marathon.
3. She finished **first** / **last** in her first race in high school.
4. At age **39** / **43**, she decided to make some changes in her life.
5. The most difficult thing for her was the **training** / **stress**.

3 Writing A dream come true

A **Think of a dream that came true for you. Answer the questions.**

- What was your dream?
- Why was it a dream for you?
- How did your dream come true?

B **Write about your dream. Use the model and your answers in Part A to help you.**

My Dream

My dream was to study Mexican cooking in Oaxaca. I loved to cook, but I wasn't a very good cook. So I went to Oaxaca to study Mexican cooking. I took a two-week class. It was a dream come true. Now I can make great meals. Who knows? I might become a chef someday.

C GROUP WORK **Share your writing. Ask and answer questions for more information.**

4 Speaking Dream planner

A **Complete the chart with a dream for the future. Then add three things you'll need to do to achieve it.**

My Dream	How I'll make it happen
	1
	2
	3

B GROUP WORK **Tell your group about your dream and how you'll achieve it.**

A: My dream is to start my own business someday.

B: That's a great dream. How will you make it happen?

A: Well, first I'll go back to school. Then I'll get a job to get some experience.

I can discuss my dreams for the future. ✓

Wrap-up

1 Quick pair review

Lesson A **Brainstorm!**

Make a list of personal goals that people can have. How many do you know? You have two minutes.

Lesson B **Do you remember?**

Write B for ways to react to bad news. Write G for ways to react to good news. You have one minute.

1 ______ That's too bad.

2 ______ I'm sorry to hear that.

3 ______ That's wonderful!

4 ______ I'm happy to hear that!

5 ______ That's a shame.

6 ______ That's great to hear!

Lesson C **Find out!**

What are two things both you and your partner think you will do in the future? Take turns. You and your partner have two minutes.

A: *I think I'll go to college in two years.*

B: *I don't think I will. I may travel first.*

Lesson D **Guess!**

Describe a dream you had when you were a child. Can your partner guess what it was? Take turns. You and your partner have two minutes.

A: *I loved swimming. I wanted to win a gold medal.*

B: *Did you want to swim in the Olympics?*

A: *Yes, I did.*

2 In the real world

What future goals do famous people have? Do you think they will achieve them? Go online and find information in English about a famous person in one of these categories. Then write about him or her.

an actor	an athlete	a businessperson	a politician	a scientist	a singer

Bill Gates

Bill Gates wants to improve people's health.

I think he'll achieve this goal . . .

Favorites

GROUP WORK **Play the game. Put a small object on *Start*. Toss a coin.**

 Move 1 space.
Heads

 Move 2 spaces.
Tails

Use the correct form of *be* to ask and answer questions. Can you answer the questions? Take turns.

Yes → Move ahead. No ← Move back.

A: *Are you interested in travel?*

B: *Yes, I am. I'm interested in new places.*

START	______ you interested in travel?	 Who ______ your favorite singer?	______ your friends interested in politics?
 Who ______ your favorite artist?	 What ______ your favorite drink?	What ______ your favorite food?	 What ______ your favorite day of the week?
 What ______ your favorite song?	 ______ you interested in fashion?	What ______ your favorite book?	______ your teacher interested in sports?
FINISH	 What ______ your favorite place for vacation?	______ your grandparents interested in technology?	 What ______ your favorite animal?

An active class?

A Add two things to the chart.

Find someone who . . .	Name	Extra information
goes to the gym		
plays table tennis		
does gymnastics		
plays soccer on the weekends		
plays a sport with a family member		
exercises in the morning		
watches baseball on TV		
listens to sports on the radio		
dislikes sports		

B CLASS ACTIVITY **Find classmates who do each thing. Ask more questions. Write their name and extra information you hear.**

A: *Do you go to the gym, Anna?*
B: *Yes, I do. I go three times a week.*
A: *Really? What do you do there?*
B: *I do yoga, and I swim.*

Help box
How often do you . . .?
Where do you . . .?
Who do you . . . with?
What's your favorite . . .?

C PAIR WORK **Share your information.**

A: *Anna goes to the gym three times a week.*
B: *Really? What does she do there?*

unit **2** Lesson A

Are you confident?

A **PAIR WORK** **Take the quiz. Take turns asking and answering the questions.**

1 What colors do you often wear?
- a I wear red, pink, and orange.
- b I wear yellow and green.
- c I wear blue and purple.
- d I wear black, white, and gray.

2 What are you like around your friends?
- a I'm always very talkative.
- b I'm talkative, but sometimes I'm quiet.
- c I'm usually the quiet one.
- d I don't know.

3 How do you enter a party?
- a I walk in and say hello to everyone.
- b I walk in and say hello to one person.
- c I walk in and look for a friend.
- d I walk in and stand in a corner.

4 You meet someone new. What do you do?
- a I say hello and ask questions.
- b I say "hi" and wait for questions.
- c I just smile.
- d I look away.

5 You see someone you like. What do you do?
- a I walk up and say hello.
- b I ask a friend to introduce us.
- c I smile at the person.
- d I do nothing.

6 The teacher asks a question. What do you do?
- a I shout out the answer.
- b I raise my hand.
- c I check my answer with a friend.
- d I look down at my desk.

B **PAIR WORK** **Add up and score your quizzes. Are the results true for you?**

A: I got 17 points.

B: You're very confident.

A: Really? I'm not sure about that.

a answers = 3 points	**c** answers = 1 point
b answers = 2 points	**d** answers = 0 points

12–18	You are very confident. Aren't you ever shy?
6–11	You are confident, but not about everything.
0–5	You're not very confident. Believe in yourself!

Find the differences

Student A

PAIR WORK You and your partner have pictures of the same people, but six things are different. Describe the pictures and ask questions to find the differences. Circle them.

A: In my picture, Brian is young. Is he young in your picture?

B: Yeah, so that's the same. In my picture, he has short straight hair.

A: Mine, too. What color is . . .?

unit **3** **Lesson A**

What's the weather like?

Student A

A **PAIR WORK** **You and your partner have information about the weather in four cities, but some information is missing. Ask questions to get the information.**

A: When is spring in Lisbon?

B: It's from March to June. What's the weather like in the spring?

A: It's warm and sunny.

Lisbon, Portugal	Season	Months	Weather
	Spring	March-June	warm and sunny
	Summer	June-September	
	Fall	September-December	
	Winter	December-March	cool and rainy

Seoul, South Korea	Season	Months	Weather
	Spring	March-June	
	Summer	June-September	hot and rainy
	Fall	September-December	
	Winter	December-March	very cold, snowy

Sydney, Australia	Season	Months	Weather
	Spring	September-December	warm and sunny
	Summer	December-March	
	Fall	March-June	
	Winter	June-September	cool and windy

Buenos Aires, Argentina	Season	Months	Weather
	Spring	September-December	
	Summer	December-March	sometimes hot, not rainy
	Fall	March-June	
	Winter	June-September	cold, not rainy

B **PAIR WORK** **Which city's seasons are similar to yours?**

Find the differences

Student B

PAIR WORK You and your partner have pictures of the same people, but six things are different. Describe the pictures and ask questions to find the differences. Circle them.

A: In my picture, Brian is young. Is he young in your picture?

B: Yeah, so that's the same. In my picture, he has short straight hair.

A: Mine, too. What color is . . .?

What's the weather like?

Student B

A **PAIR WORK** **You and your partner have information about the weather in four cities, but some information is missing. Ask questions to get the information.**

A: When is spring in Lisbon?

B: It's from March to June. What's the weather like in the spring?

A: It's warm and sunny.

Lisbon, Portugal	Season	Months	Weather
	Spring	March-June	
	Summer	June-September	hot, not rainy
	Fall	September-December	warm and windy
	Winter	December-March	

Seoul, South Korea	Season	Months	Weather
	Spring	March-June	warm, not rainy
	Summer	June-September	
	Fall	September-December	sunny and cool
	Winter	December-March	

Sydney, Australia	Season	Months	Weather
	Spring	September-December	
	Summer	December-March	hot and dry
	Fall	March-June	cool and rainy
	Winter	June-September	

Buenos Aires, Argentina	Season	Months	Weather
	Spring	September-December	warm and rainy
	Summer	December-March	
	Fall	March-June	rainy, not cool
	Winter	June-September	

B **PAIR WORK** **Which city's seasons are similar to yours?**

Someday . . .

A Write information about things you'd like to do someday.

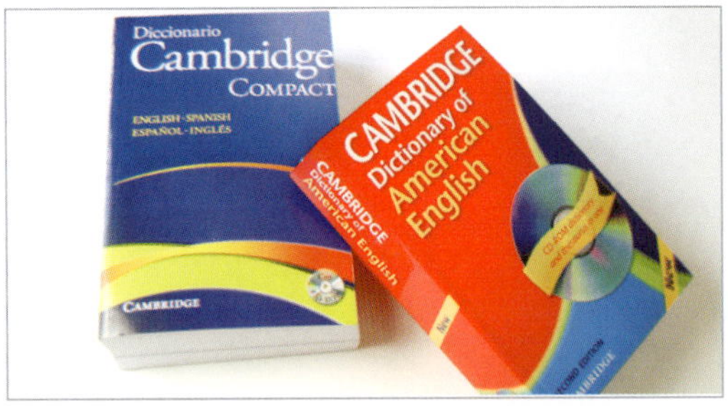

a language I'd like to learn: ____________

a person I'd like to meet: ____________

a country I'd like to visit: ____________

a job I'd like to have: ____________

something I'd like to buy: ____________

a sport I'd like to try: ____________

a place I'd like to live: ____________

a game I'd like to play: ____________

B GROUP WORK **Share your ideas. Ask and answer questions for more information.**

A: I think I'd like to learn Spanish someday.

B: Really? Why?

A: Because I'd like to visit Costa Rica.

unit 4 Lesson A

Home sweet home

A PAIR WORK **Look at the picture for two minutes. Try to remember the rooms, furniture, and other details.**

B PAIR WORK **Cover the picture. Ask and answer these questions. What do you remember?**

- How many rooms are there in the house?
- Which rooms are on the first floor? the second floor?
- How much light is there in the living room? How many windows are there?
- Is there much furniture in the living room? What's there?
- What's on the coffee table? What's on the kitchen table?
- Are there many pictures in the house? Where are they?
- How are the two bedrooms different?
- How are the two bathrooms different?
- Is there much space in this house? Do you think there is much noise?

A: *How many rooms are there in the house?*

B: *I think there are . . . rooms.*

A: *I think so, too. Which rooms are on the first floor?*

C **Look at the picture again and check your answers.**

Cleanup time

PAIR WORK You need to do some chores around the apartment. Decide who does each chore. Be fair!

A: *Could you take out the garbage?*

B: *Sure. I can take it out. Would you clean out the closet?*

Don't get up!

Student A

A PAIR WORK **Tell your partner to cover the pictures. Describe the exercises. Your partner does the actions. Take turns.**

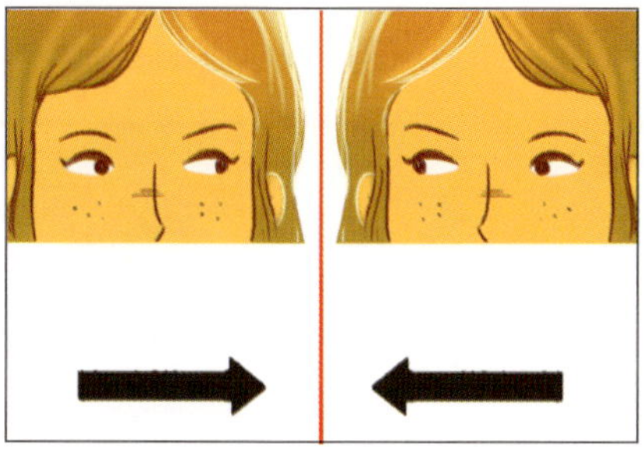

Eye exercises
Move your eyes quickly to the right. Then move them quickly to the left. Repeat five times.

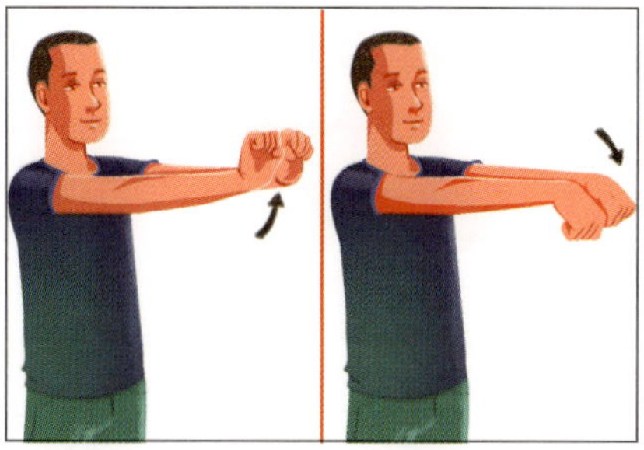

Wrist exercises
Stretch your arms in front of you. Move your hands up and down quickly. Repeat five times.

Shoulder exercises
Lift your shoulders slowly to your ears. Don't move, and hold for three seconds. Then lower your shoulders. Repeat three times.

A: *Move your eyes to the right.*
B: *Like this?*
A: *Yes. Now move them to the left.*

B PAIR WORK **How did your partner do? How does your partner feel?**

Student B

A PAIR WORK **Tell your partner to cover the pictures. Describe the exercises. Your partner does the actions. Take turns.**

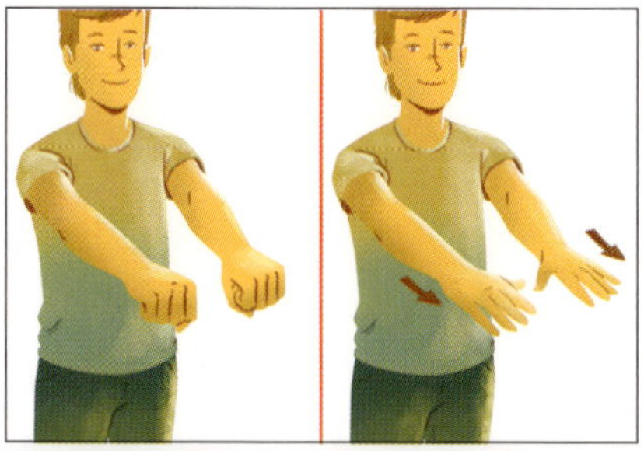

Hand exercises
Stretch your arms in front of you. Close your hands. Then open your hands quickly. Repeat five times.

Neck exercises
Touch your right ear to your right shoulder. Then touch your left ear to your left shoulder. Repeat five times.

Arm exercises
Lift your right arm up and down. Then lift your left arm up and down. Repeat three times.

B: *Stretch your arms in front of you.*
A: *Like this?*
B: *Yes. Now close your hands.*

B **How did your partner do? How does your partner feel?**

How healthy are you?

A PAIR WORK **Take the quiz. Take turns asking and answering the questions.**

1 How many servings of fruit and vegetables do you eat a day?

- ☐ a Five or more
- ☐ b Three to four
- ☐ c One to two

2 How often do you eat breakfast?

- ☐ a Every day
- ☐ b Two to six times a week
- ☐ c Rarely

3 How many meals do you eat a day?

- ☐ a Four or five small meals
- ☐ b Three meals
- ☐ c One or two big meals

4 How much junk food do you eat?

- ☐ a Very little
- ☐ b About average
- ☐ c A lot

5 How often do you exercise?

- ☐ a Every day
- ☐ b Two or three times a week
- ☐ c Never

6 How long do you spend watching TV or playing video games each week?

- ☐ a One to two hours
- ☐ b Three to six hours
- ☐ c Seven or more hours

7 How well do you sleep at night?

- ☐ a Very well
- ☐ b Pretty well
- ☐ c Not very well

8 How often do you get a checkup?

- ☐ a Once a year
- ☐ b Every two or three years
- ☐ c Hardly ever

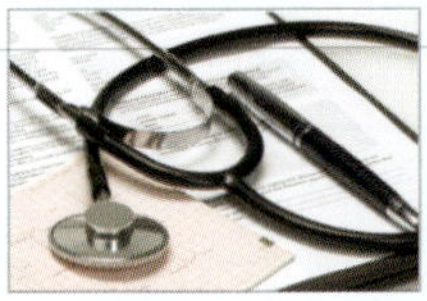

9 How happy are you with your health?

- ☐ a Very happy
- ☐ b Pretty happy
- ☐ c Not very happy

a answers = 3 points
b answers = 2 points
c answers = 1 point
21–27 You're very healthy. Congratulations!
15–20 You're pretty healthy. Keep it up!
9–14 You can improve your health. Start now!

B PAIR WORK **Add up and score your quizzes. Are the results true for you? Why or why not?**

A: My score is 16. It says I'm pretty healthy. I think that's true.

B: My score is 20, but I think I'm very healthy.

unit **6** # Lesson A

TV listings

A PAIR WORK **Look at the TV listings. What types of shows are they?**

	Channel 4	Channel 11	Channel 13
7:00–7:30	**Win or Lose** Everyone's favorite game show! Play at home!	**Soap Stars on Ice** See your favorite soap stars ice skate for charity!	**Man's Best Friend** The new sitcom about a talking horse named Fred
7:30–8:00	**Under Arrest** Police drama starring Damien Porter		**Travels with Ryan** This week, Ryan learns how to samba in Brazil.
8:00–8:30	**Mr. and Mrs. Right** The best reality show on TV! Vote for your favorite couple!	**The Year in Sports** The best baseball moments of the year	**The Ina Lopez Show** Tough questions, honest answers. Tonight talk-show queen Ina takes your calls!
8:30–9:00		**Meet My Family** A funny family sitcom	
9:00–9:30	**Lions of Kenya** "An amazing documentary"	**Take It or Leave It** Part game show, part reality show. New!	**My Roommate Ralph** A new sitcom from the creators of *Alien Mom*
9:30–10:00	**The News** Local news with Dinah and Jim	**Family Life** The funny new cartoon for adults	**Kiss and Tell** See the soap everyone is talking about!

B PAIR WORK **Look at the information about the Green family. They have only one TV. What shows can they watch together from 7:00 to 10:00?**

Dan Green
- enjoys watching sports and news
- hates to watch reality shows

Sarah Green
- hopes to visit Rio de Janeiro
- prefers to watch funny shows

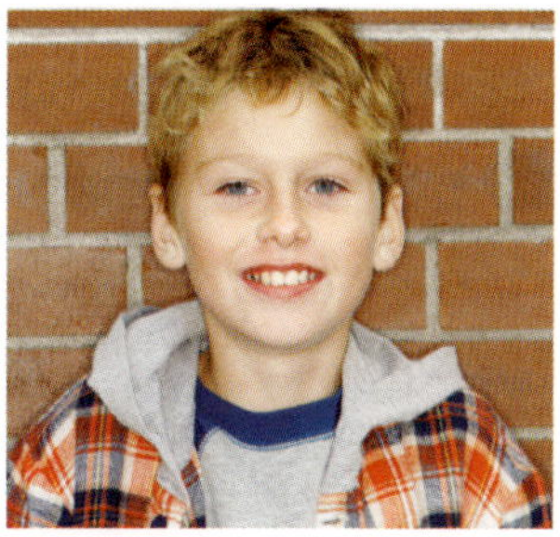

Rick Green
- loves to watch game shows hates soap operas

Rose Green
- enjoys watching soap operas
- doesn't like watching sitcoms

A: They can watch *Win or Lose* at 7:00. Rick loves to watch game shows.

B: And they can watch *Travels with Ryan* at 7:30. Sarah hopes to visit Brazil.

C GROUP WORK **What shows do you want to watch?**

My daily planner

A **Make a schedule for tomorrow afternoon and evening. Use the ideas below and your own ideas. Write four activities in the daily planner. Think about how long each activity will take.**

go grocery shopping	meet friends for coffee	watch a movie on TV
watch sports with friends	chat online with friends	clean my room
exercise at the gym	watch the news	study at the library
__________	__________	__________

Date: / / Sun Mon Tues Wed Thurs Fri Sat	Notes	Date: / / Sun Mon Tues Wed Thurs Fri Sat	Notes
2:00		6:00	
2:30		6:30	
3:00		7:00	
3:30		7:30	
4:00		8:00	
4:30		8:30	
5:00		9:00	
5:30		9:30	

B CLASS ACTIVITY **Think of three fun activities. Find classmates who want to do the activities with you. Add the information to your planners.**

A: *What are you doing tomorrow evening at 7:00?*
B: *I'm meeting some friends for coffee.*
A: *Oh, OK. Do you want to see a movie at 8:00?*
B: *I'd love to, but I can't. I'm . . .*

Which product is . . .?

A PAIR WORK **Add two more products to the chart. Then think of two examples you know for each product and write their names in the chart.**

	Example 1	Example 2	
Video game			Which is newer? Which is more fun? Which is . . .?
Computer			Which is easier to use? Which is faster? Which is . . .?
Cell phone			Which is thinner? Which is less expensive? Which is . . .?
Car			Which is smaller? Which is faster? Which is . . .?

B **Compare each pair of products. Use the questions in Part A and your own ideas.**

A: I think . . . is newer than . . .

B: That's right. It's more fun, too.

A: I don't really agree. I think . . . is more fun. My friends and I can play it all day!

C **Share your comparisons with the class. Which product is better? Why?**

They aren't big enough!

Student A

PAIR WORK You and your partner have pictures of the same people, but there are eight differences. Describe the pictures and ask questions about the differences. Circle them.

A: In my picture, Nancy's pants are too baggy. They look very uncomfortable.

B: In my picture, Nancy's pants are too tight. So, that's different.

A: What about Maria's pants? I think they're too short.

B: They're too short in my picture, too. So, that's the same.

unit **9** Lesson A

From the past

Student A

A PAIR WORK **You and your partner have information on six famous people from the past, but some information is missing. Ask these questions and complete the information.**

- Where was . . . born?
- When was . . . born?
- What did . . . do?
- Why was . . . famous?

Name	**George Washington**	**Frida Kahlo**	**Charlie Chaplin**
Place of birth	the U.S.	Mexico	England
Date of birth	February 22, 1732	July 6, 1907	____________
What did	____________	painter	actor and director
Why famous	He was the first president of the U.S.	She was very ________, and her art was ________.	He was in a lot of funny black-and-white movies.

Name	**Jesse Owens**	**Marie Curie**	**Yuri Gagarin**
Place of birth	the U.S.	____________	Russia
Date of birth	September 12, 1913	November 7, 1867	March 9, 1934
What did	athlete	scientist	astronaut
Why famous	He was the first American to win ________ gold ________ in track and field in one Olympics.	She was the first person to win two Nobel prizes.	He was the first person in ____________.

B PAIR WORK **Look at the information. What similarities can you find between these famous people and other famous people you know?**

unit **8** # Lesson A

What can you do here?

A **PAIR WORK** **Think about where you live. Where can you do each of these things? Take notes.**

hear live music

see interesting dance

buy fun souvenirs

eat good, cheap food

see statues and art

enjoy beautiful views

go for a walk

visit historical sites

enjoy nature

A: You can often hear live music at the city square.

B: Right. And there's also the university coffee shop.

A: That's true. They have live music on Fridays and Saturdays.

B **GROUP WORK** **Share your information. How similar are your ideas?**

unit **8** # Lesson C

City quiz

A PAIR WORK **Take the quiz. Ask the questions and guess the answers. Take turns.**

1 What is the biggest city in North America?
   a Mexico City b Los Angeles c Washington, D.C.

2 Where is the biggest soccer stadium in South America?
   a Buenos Aires, Argentina b Rio de Janeiro, Brazil c Lima, Peru

3 "The Big Apple" is the nickname for what U.S. city?
   a Boston b Washington, D.C. c New York City

4 Which city is on the Han River?
   a New Orleans, U.S. b Venice, Italy c Seoul, South Korea

5 What is the most expensive city?
   a Tokyo, Japan b London, England c Rome, Italy

6 What is the safest big city in the U.S.?
   a New York City b Las Vegas c Boston

7 The oldest subway system in the world is in what European city?
   a Paris, France b Madrid, Spain c London, England

8 Which city has the worst traffic in the U.S.?
   a Chicago b Los Angeles c San Francisco

9 What city is in both Europe and Asia?
   a Berlin, Germany b Stockholm, Sweden c Istanbul, Turkey

10 The biggest public square in the world is in what city?
   a Beijing, China b Moscow, Russia c London, England

B **Check your answers on the bottom of this page. How many did you get correct?**

C PAIR WORK **Think of another question and three possible answer choices. Ask another pair. Do they know the answer?**

"What's the largest city in . . .?"

1. a 2. b 3. c 4. c 5. a 6. a 7. c 8. b 9. c 10. a

They aren't big enough!

Student B

PAIR WORK **You and your partner have pictures of the same people, but there are eight differences. Describe the pictures and ask questions about the differences. Circle them.**

A: In my picture, Nancy's pants are too baggy. They look very uncomfortable.

B: In my picture, Nancy's pants are too tight. So, that's different.

A: What about Maria's pants? I think they're too short.

B: They're too short in my picture, too. So, that's the same.

From the Past

Student B

A PAIR WORK **You and your partner have information about six famous people from the past, but some information is missing. Ask these questions and complete the information.**

- Where was . . . born?
- When was . . . born?
- What did . . . do?
- Why was . . . famous?

Name	George Washington	Frida Kahlo	Charlie Chaplin
Place of birth	the U.S.	________	England
Date of birth	February 22, 1732	July 6, 1907	April 16, 1889
What did	politician	painter	actor and director
Why famous	He was the first ________ of the ________.	She was very creative, and her art was very interesting.	He was in a lot of ________ black-and-white ________.

Name	Jesse Owens	Marie Curie	Yuri Gagarin
Place of birth	the U.S.	Poland	Russia
Date of birth	________	November 7, 1867	March 9, 1934
What did	athlete	scientist	________
Why famous	He was the first American to win four gold medals in track and field in one Olympics.	She was the first person to win ________ Nobel ________.	He was the first person in space.

B PAIR WORK **Look at the information. What similarities can you find between these famous people and other famous people you know?**

unit 9 Lesson C

What an inspiring person!

A **Think of three people you admire. Use the categories below or think of your own. Then complete the chart.**

an athlete	a musician	a writer	an artist	a scientist
a politician	an actor/actress	a business leader	a family member	a teacher

	Name	Why	Notes
1			
2			
3			

B GROUP WORK **Share your ideas. Ask and answer questions for more information.**

A: I really admire Sergey Brin and Larry Page. They started Google.

B: Why do you admire them?

A: Well, I think they're both talented and intelligent.

C: Do you think they're also . . .?

C **Is there a famous person who you *don't* admire? Why not?**

A one-of-a-kind menu

A GROUP WORK **Imagine you're going to open a restaurant together. Answer the questions and create a menu.**

- What's the name of your restaurant?
- What do you want to serve?
- Is it a cheap or an expensive restaurant? Write the prices.

______________ **Restaurant**

APPETIZERS

______________ ______
______________ ______
______________ ______
______________ ______
______________ ______

MAIN DISHES

______________ ______
______________ ______
______________ ______
______________ ______
______________ ______

SIDE DISHES

______________ ______
______________ ______
______________ ______
______________ ______
______________ ______

DESSERTS

______________ ______
______________ ______
______________ ______
______________ ______
______________ ______

DRINKS

______________ ______ ______________ ______
______________ ______ ______________ ______

A: Let's have three or four appetizers.

B: OK. How about some garlic bread and onion soup?

C: That sounds good. Let's have a salad, too. How about . . .?

B GROUP WORK **Exchange your menus. Ask and answer questions about the items. Which dishes would you order?**

A: The Mexican salad sounds interesting. What's in it?

B: It has lettuce, tomatoes, onions, peppers, beans, and corn.

Yes, I have.

GROUP WORK **Play the game. Put a small object on *Start*. Toss a coin.**

 Move 1 space.

Heads

 Move 2 spaces.

Tails

Use the words to ask and answer questions. Ask your own *Have you ever . . .?* questions on the **Free question** spaces. Take turns.

A: Have you ever made French fries?

B: Yes, I have.

START	Have / ever / make French fries?	Have / ever / cook a meal for another person? 	Have / ever / try Thai food?
Have / ever / eat Indian food? 	Free question	Have / ever / bake cookies? 	Have / ever / make popcorn?
Free question	Have / ever / have breakfast in bed? 	Have / ever / eat at the beach?	Have / ever / have a terrible stomachache? 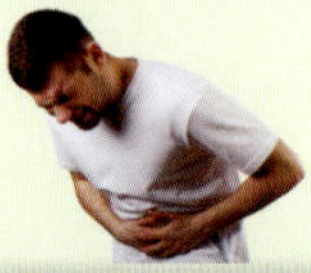
Have / ever / have a really expensive meal?	Free question	Have / ever / be to a Korean restaurant? 	Have / ever / drink coffee late at night? 
Have / ever / watch a cooking show on TV?	Have / ever / have a picnic? 	Free question	FINISH

Movie favorites

A Complete the chart with six types of movies that you like. Add a title for each type.

	Type of movie	Title of movie
1		
2		
3		
4		
5		
6		

B CLASS ACTIVITY Find classmates who like the same types of movies you like. Then ask questions with *Have you ever . . . ?*

A: I really like animated movies.

B: So do I.

A: Really? Have you ever seen *Despicable Me?*

B: Yes, I have. I love that movie!

Class Survey

A **Complete the questions with your own ideas.**

1 Do you like the band ______________ ? ☐
(a band)

2 Do you like the song ______________ ? ☐
(a song title)

3 Do you have the album ______________ ? ☐
(name of an album)

4 Do you ever listen to ______________ ? ☐
(a type of music)

5 Do you know the words to the song ______________ ? ☐
(name of a song)

6 Did you listen to ______________ as a child? ☐
(a type of music)

7 Would you like to see ______________ in concert? ☐
(a singer or band)

B **CLASS ACTIVITY** **Ask your classmates the questions in Part A. How many people said "yes" to each question? Write the total number in the boxes.**

C **PAIR WORK** **Share your information.**

A: *A lot of our classmates like the band . . .*

B: *That's interesting. Not many of us like the band . . .*

D **Share the most interesting information with the class.**

"All of us would like to see . . . in concert."

Why did I do that?

A **Think about things that you did in the past. Check (✓) the things in the first column that are true for you. Then add three more things.**

- ☐ I took a long trip to ________.
- ☐ I sent a text to someone to ________.
- ☐ I took a test to ________.
- ☐ I joined a gym to ________.
- ☐ I got a cell phone to ________.
- ☐ I uploaded some photos to ________.
- ☐ I worked hard to ________.
- ☐ I got a part time job to ________.
- ☐ ________ to ________.
- ☐ ________ to ________.
- ☐ ________ to ________.

B **Why did you do each thing? Complete the sentences in Part A with an infinitive of purpose. Use the ideas below or think of your own.**

talk with my friends	learn an instrument	show my friends
get my driver's license	get some experience	get a job
share good news	buy a gift	make more friends
save money	lose weight	see my relatives

C **GROUP WORK** **Share your sentences. Ask and answer questions for more information.**

A: *I took a long trip to see my relatives.*

B: *When was that?*

A: *Last year.*

C: *Where did you go?*

A: *I went . . .*

Next year . . .

A **Add two future activities to the chart.**

Do you think you'll . . . next year?	Name	Other details
take a trip with your family		
start a new hobby		
join a gym		
get married		
buy something expensive		
move to a different home		
start a career		
learn a musical instrument		

B **CLASS ACTIVITY** **Find classmates who will do each thing. Write their names. Ask and answer questions for more information. Take notes.**

A: *Jun, do you think you'll take a trip with your family next year?*

B: *Yes, I do.*

A: *Really? Where will you go?*

B: *We're planning to go to Australia to visit some friends. I hope to . . .*

C **GROUP WORK** **Share the most interesting information.**

Irregular verbs

Base form	Simple past	Past Participle
be	was, were	been
become	became	become
build	built	built
buy	bought	bought
choose	chose	chosen
come	came	come
do	did	done
draw	drew	drawn
drink	drank	drunk
drive	drove	driven
eat	ate	eaten
feel	felt	felt
get	got	gotten
give	gave	given
go	went	gone
hang	hung	hung
have	had	had
hear	heard	heard
hold	held	held
know	knew	known
leave	left	left
lose	lost	lost
make	made	made

Base form	Simple past	Past Participle
meet	met	met
pay	paid	paid
put	put	put
read	read	read
ride	rode	ridden
run	ran	run
say	said	said
see	saw	seen
sell	sold	sold
send	sent	sent
sing	sang	sung
sit	sat	sat
sleep	slept	slept
speak	spoke	spoken
spend	spent	spent
stand	stood	stood
swim	swam	swum
take	took	taken
teach	taught	taught
think	thought	thought
wear	wore	worn
win	won	won
write	wrote	written

Credits

The authors and publishers acknowledge the following sources of copyright material and are grateful for the permissions granted. While every effort has been made, it has not always been possible to identify the sources of all the material used, or to trace all copyright holders. If any omissions are brought to our notice, we will be happy to include the appropriate acknowledgements on reprinting and in the next update to the digital edition, as applicable.

Photography
All below images are sourced from Getty Images.
Front Matter: Hero Images; **U1:** Rob Ball/WireImage; Maxiphoto/iStock/Getty Images Plus; pashapixel/iStock/Getty Images Plus; empire331/iStock/Getty Images Plus; Shuji Kobayashi/The Image Bank; tioloco/iStock/Getty Images Plus; artisteer/iStock/Getty Images Plus; Javier Pierini/The Image Bank; Digital Vision; KidStock/Blend Images; 4x6/ iStock/Getty Images Plus; Kris Timken/Blend Images; Patrik Giardino/Corbis; BakiBG/E+; Donald Miralle/DigitalVision; Robert Daly/OJO Images; Gary Burchell/DigitalVision; Andrew Errington/Photographer's Choice; EXTREME-PHOTOGRAPHER/E+; Thinkstock/ Stockbyte; digitalfarmer/iStock/Getty Images Plus; Westend61; JGI/Jamie Grill/Blend Images; Hannah Foslien/Getty Images Sport; **U2:** Alexander Spatari/Moment; Mark Edward Atkinson/Tracey Lee/Blend Images; JGI/Jamie Grill/Blend Images; Blue Images/ Corbis; Wavebreakmedia/iStock/Getty Images Plus; Asia Images Group; KaVaStudio2015/iStock/Getty Images Plus; PeopleImages/E+; Purestock; Tanya Constantine/Blend Images; alvarez/E+; Firda Beka; Ronnie Kaufman/Larry Hirshowitz/ Blend Images; Image Source; Dominique Charriau/WireImage; **U3:** Andersen Ross/ DigitalVision; gpointstudio/iStock/Getty Images Plus; Mats Silvan/Moment; technotr/ Vetta; VV-pics/iStock/Getty Images Plus; Cultura RM Exclusive/Philip Lee Harvey/Cultura Exclusive; JodiJacobson/E+; Glowimages; Georgia Immins/EyeEm; Getty Images; Alex Robinson/robertharding; Robert Francis/robertharding; Fouque/iStock/Getty Images Plus; Andrew Lichtenstein/Corbis News; sebastianosecondi/iStock/Getty Images Plus; Shannon Fagan; pavlen/iStock/Getty Images Plus; RichLegg/iStock/Getty Images Plus; Peter Dennen; Chris Speedie; Raimund Linke; hudiemm/iStock/Getty Images Plus; Denyshutter/iStock/Getty Images Plus; PhotoObjects.net/Getty Images Plus; Comstock/ Stockbyte; Martin Moos/Lonely Planet Images; Chen Liu/EyeEm; **U4:** Jumping Rocks; arnitorfason/iStock/Getty Images Plus; dabldy/iStock Editorial/Getty Images Plus; PETER COOK/Corbis Documentary; JazzIRT/E+; Chefmd/iStock/Getty Images Plus; ennesseePhotographer/iStock Editorial/Getty Images Plus; Gunter Marx Photography/ Corbis Documentary; Tatjana Kaufmann; John Rensten/The Image Bank; Siri Stafford/ DigitalVision; hulya-erkisi/iStock/Getty Images Plus; Eerik/iStock/Getty Images Plus; fStop Images - Patrick Strattner/Brand X Pictures; TommL/iStock/Getty Images Plus; Eco Images/Universal Images Group; shironosov/iStock/Getty Images Plus; **U5:** Jupiterimages/Pixland/Getty Images Plus; Matthieu Spohn/PhotoAlto Agency RF Collections; Niedring/Drentwett/MITO images; RichVintage/E+; Purestock; Westend61; Peathegee Inc/Blend Images; Hola Images; YKD/iStock/Getty Images Plus; kellllI/iStock/ Getty Images Plus; energyy/iStock/Getty Images Plus; drbimages/E+; zegers06/iStock/ Getty Images Plus; Peter Dazeley/Photographer's Choice; dima_sidelnikov/iStock/Getty Images Plus; laindiapiaroa/Blend Images/Getty Images Plus; Highwaystarz-Photography/iStock/Getty Images Plus; Eva-Katalin/E+; bagotaj/iStock/Getty Images Plus; Clerkenwell/Vetta; Tom Merton/OJO Images; South_agency/iStock/Getty Images Plus; B. Boissonnet; paylessimages/iStock/Getty Images Plus; hxdbzxy/iStock/Getty Images Plus; Image Source/Photodisc; Jose Luis Pelaez Inc/Blend Images; Dougal Waters/DigitalVision; Brand X; Leanna Rathkelly/Leanna Rathkelly; Hero Images; shironosov/iStock/Getty Images Plus; Robert van 't Hoenderdaal/iStock Editorial/Getty Images Plus; Simon McGill/Moment; Lucinda Newton-Dunn/Moment; Peter Dazeley/ Photographer's Choice; Velvetfish/iStock/Getty Images Plus; undefined/iStock/Getty Images Plus; onepony/iStock/Getty Images Plus; Olga_k_/iStock/Getty Images Plus; studiocasper/iStock/Getty Images Plus; Pascal Broze/ONOKY; **U6:** Fernando Trabanco Fotografía/Moment; Tara Moore/Corbis; Jacob Wackerhausen/iStock/Getty Images Plus; Chris Ryan/Caiaimage; BJI/Blue Jean Images; Alija/Vetta; Lorado/E+; DreamPictures/ Stone; Chud/Moment; Andy Rouse/The Image Bank; Erik Dreyer/Stone; powerofforever/ E+; simonkr/E+; Vicki Jauron, Babylon and Beyond/Moment; SÃbastien RABANY/ Photononstop; Charley Gallay/Getty Images Entertainment; hikesterson/iStock/Getty Images Plus; RUNSTUDIO/DigitalVision; Car Culture ® Collection; **U7:** Kathrin Ziegler/ Taxi; Mike Watson Images/moodboard/Getty Images Plus; gradyreese/E+; Thomas Barwick/Photodisc; Jeff Greenberg/Universal Images Group; anyaberkut/iStock/Getty Images Plus; Nerthuz/iStock/Getty Images Plus; Dieter Spears/EyeEm; 3dgoksu/iStock/ Getty Images Plus; 3drenderings/iStock/Getty Images Plus; Marco Rosario Venturini Autieri/iStock/Getty Images Plus; luismmolina/iStock/Getty Images Plus; ZargonDesign/ E+; Chris Collins/Corbis; Vincenzo Lombardo/Photodisc; cleotis/iStock/Getty Images Plus; pongky.n/iStock/Getty Images Plus; nevodka/iStock/Getty Images Plus; ItsraSanprasert/iStock/Getty Images Plus; MarkELaw/iStock/Getty Images Plus; Paolo_ Toffanin/iStock/Getty Images Plus; digitalskillet/iStock/Getty Images Plus; naumoid/ iStock/Getty Images Plus; richjem/iStock/Getty Images Plus; rasslava/iStock/Getty Images Plus; arogant/iStock/Getty Images Plus; momcilog/iStock/Getty Images Plus; emreogan/iStock/Getty Images Plus; lypnyk2/iStock/Getty Images Plus; Wulf Voss/ EyeEm; Tarzhanova/iStock/Getty Images Plus; panic_attack/iStock/Getty Images Plus; Vasilina Popova/The Image Bank; Chen Chao; Maremagnum/Photolibrary; Martin_ Szczepaniak/iStock Editorial/Getty Images Plus; DC_Colombia/iStock Editorial/Getty Images Plus; **U8:** guruXOOX/iStock/Getty Images Plus; Westend61; FotoDuets/iStock Editorial/Getty Images Plus; csfotoimages/iStock Editorial/Getty Images Plus; Sergio J. Pitamitz/Corbis Documentary; imantsu/iStock/Getty Images Plus; rachel/iStock/Getty Images Plus; Martin Wahlborg/iStock/Getty Images Plus; Ed-Ni-Photo/iStock Editorial/ Getty Images Plus; Richard T. Nowitz/Corbis Documentary; bluejayphoto/iStock Editorial/Getty Images Plus; VitalyEdush/iStock/Getty Images Plus; baona/iStock/Getty Images Plus; Lonely Planet Images; Jose Fuste Raga/Corbis Documentary; shomos uddin/Moment; Dmitry Ageev/Blend Images; Neale Clark/robertharding; BRANDONJ74/ E+; Carlos Ciudad Photos/Moment; Maskot; Wei Fang/Moment; **U9:** Michael Gottschalk/ Photothek; Pablo Cuadra/Getty Images Entertainment; Mehdi Taamallah/NurPhoto; Kelvin Ma/Bloomberg; Jason LaVeris/FilmMagic; RG-vc/iStock/Getty Images Plus; kickers/iStock/Getty Images Plus; bjones27/E+; Martin Hartley/The Image Bank; Jupiterimages/Goodshoot/Getty Images Plus; STR/AFP; DreamPictures/Blend Images; skynesher/E+; Comstock Images/Stockbyte; VANDERLEI ALMEIDA/AFP; ben radford/ Corbis Sport; George Hoyningen-Huene/Condé Nast Collection; Library of Congress/ Corbis Historical/VCG; David Levenson/Getty Images Entertainment; JOSE CENDON/AFP; Bettmann; Mahmoud Khaled/Anadolu Agency; THOMAS COEX/AFP; Chris Ratcliffe/ Bloomberg; Wavebreakmedia; **U10:** Blulz60/iStock Editorial/Getty Images Plus; Sunwoo Jung/DigitalVision; Katie Garrod/AWL Images; Jon Hicks/Corbis Documentary; effrey Greenberg/Universal Images Group; Photodisc; Cristina Cassinelli; James Baigrie; Asia Images Group; HariKarki2003/iStock/Getty Images Plus; naruedom/iStock/Getty Images Plus; mikdam/iStock/Getty Images Plus; NightAndDayImages/E+; Maximilian Stock Ltd./ Photolibrary; Amarita/iStock/Getty Images Plus; 3dsguru/iStock/Getty Images Plus; Boogich/iStock/Getty Images Plus; EmirMemedovski/E+; whitewish/iStock/Getty Images Plus; India Today Group; PeopleImages/E+; Eurngkwan/iStock/Getty Images Plus; **U11:** Hero Images; Emmanuel Faure/The Image Bank; Chad Slattery/The Image Bank; izusek/ iStock/Getty Images Plus; Egon Bömsch/imageBROKER; James Whitaker/Stone; Denkou Images/Cultura; Chud/Moment; Westend61; Hill Street Studios/Blend Images; Michael Klippfeld/Moment; mmac72/E+; Stephanie Rausser/DigitalVision; andresr/E+; Crazytang/E+; Topic Images Inc.; Ryan Smith/Corbis; olmozott98/iStock Editorial/Getty Images Plus; Rubberball/Mike Kemp; Onradio/iStock/Getty Images Plus; JGI/Tom Grill/ Blend Images; Mlenny/iStock/Getty Images Plus; Inti St. Clair/DigitalVision; Bokeshi/ iStock/Getty Images Plus; DreamPictures/Blend Images; Alexei Cruglicov/iStock/Getty Images Plus; piovesempre/iStock/Getty Images Plus; Michael Luhrenberg/iStock/Getty Images Plus; JGI/Tom Grill/Blend Images; Jose Luis Pelaez Inc/Blend Images; moodboard/Cultura; Gabriel Rossi/LatinContent WO; John Parra; BaloOm Studios/ Moment; **U12:** Kemter/iStock/Getty Images Plus; PJPhoto69/iStock/Getty Images Plus; Westend61; Glow Wellness; Rainer Holz/Corbis; shank_ali/E+; Dougal Waters/ DigitalVision; john shepherd/iStock/Getty Images Plus; Neustockimages/E+; laughingmango/iStock/Getty Images Plus; Eakachai Leesin/EyeEm; Jose Luis Pelaez Inc/ Blend Images; JGI/Tom Grill/Blend Images; Troy House/Corbis; stockyimages/iStock/ Getty Images Plus; Michael H/DigitalVision; Thinkstock Images/Stockbyte; Blend Images; Design Pics; Dirk Anschutz; Predrag Vuckovic/E+; Bellurget Jean Louis; aldomurillo/E+; fstop123/iStock/Getty Images Plus; Blend Images - JGI/Jamie Grill/Brand X Pictures; Erstudiostok/iStock/Getty Images Plus; Lucas Lenci Photo/The Image Bank; David Cannon/Allsport; John Lamparski/Getty Images Entertainment; **End Matter:** golovorez/ iStock/Getty Images Plus; afe207/iStock/Getty Images Plus; ugurv/iStock/Getty Images Plus; Doug Byrnes/Corbis; GoodLifeStudio/iStock/Getty Images Plus; C Squared Studios/ Photodisc; Raquel Pedrosa/Moment Open; Kenny McCartney/Moment; JGI/Jamie Grill/ Blend Images; Javier Pierini/The Image Bank; Purestock; YinYang/E+; skynesher/E+; Maskot; Squaredpixels/E+; Caiaimage/Paul Bradbury; Image Source/DigitalVision; PhonlamaiPhoto/iStock/Getty Images Plus; fazon1/iStock/Getty Images Plus; zhudifeng/ iStock/Getty Images Plus; miflippo/iStock/Getty Images Plus; Dougal Waters/ Photographer's Choice; Juanmonino/iStock/Getty Images Plus; Ron Levine/Stockbyte; Fuse/Corbis; Jon Feingersh/Blend Images; Igor Emmerich/Corbis/VCG/Corbis; Saro17/ E+; Brand X Pictures/Stokebyte; Sergey Nazarov/iStock/Getty Images Plus; SuperStock; Hulton Archive; Popperfoto; Barna Tanko/iStock Editorial/Getty Images Plus; John W Banagan/Photographer's Choice; WIN-Initiative; SAM YEH/AFP; Jeffrey Greenberg/ Universal Images Group; QQ7/iStock/Getty Images Plus; yogysic/DigitalVision Vectors; elenaleonova/E+; DonNichols/E+; mukesh-kumar/iStock/Getty Images Plus; Jupiterimages/Photolibrary; KatarzynaBialasiewicz/iStock/Getty Images Plus; Studio_ Dagdagaz/iStock/Getty Images Plus; bonchan/iStock/Getty Images Plus; ChesiireCat/ iStock/Getty Images Plus; Roberto Ricciuti/WireImage; Lionel LOURDEL/Photononstop; chameleonseye/iStock Editorial/Getty Images Plus; chameleonseye/iStock/Getty Images Plus; QQ7/iStock/Getty Images Plus; SuperStock; Hulton Archive; Popperfoto; Bloomberg; David R. Anchuelo/Getty Images.

Front cover by Hero Images; Eva-Katalin/E+. Back cover by Monty Rakusen/Cultura.
The following images are sourced from other libraries:
U1: Barry Mason/Alamy; Michael Matthews/Alamy; Frank Veronsky; Media Bakery; MBI/Alamy; AP/Wide World Photos; **U2:** FogStock/Alamy; Imagebroker/Alamy; Frank Veronsky; Age Fotostock; Shutterstock; Kathy deWitt/Alamy; **U3:** Shutterstock; Photo Library; Cleo Photo/Alamy; Media Bakery; Alamy; **U4:** AP/Wide World Photos; Frank Veronsky; George Kerrigan; Douglas Keister; Franck Fotos/Alamy; Shutterstock; Reuters; Alamy; Scott Jenkins; **U5:** Frank Veronsky; Alamy; **U6:** Frank Veronsky; CBS/Everett Collection; **U7:** Shutterstock; Frank Veronsky; Photo Edit; John Lander/Alamy; Alamy; **U8:** Alamy; Wendy Connett/Alamy; Shutterstock; Roger Cracknell/Alamy; Nic Cleave Photography/Alamy; Media Bakery; Terry Smith Images/Alamy; Tibor Bognar/Alamy; Scott Olson; **U9:** NASA; AP/Wide World Photos; Frank Veronsky; Pictorial Press Ltd./ Alamy; AP/Wide World Photos; Newscom; Media Bakery; AP/Wide World Photos; **U10:** Shutterstock; Bon Appetit/Alamy; Inmagine; Martin Lee/Alamy; Media Bakery; Carlos Davila/Alamy; Food Folio/Alamy; Frank Veronsky; Ninja Akasaka; Jack Carey/Alamy; **U11:** Media Bakery; Joseph De Sciose; Richard Levine/Alamy; Inmagine; **U12:** Media Bakery; Shutterstock; Yellow Dog Productions/Alamy; Frank Veronsky; Courtesy of Suzanne Lefebre; **End Matter:** Shannon99/Alamy; US mint; Age Fotostock; Media Bakery; Imagebroker/Alamy; Adventure House; Photo Stock Israel/Alamy; Shutterstock; Andrew Payne/Alamy; Everett Collection; Mary Evans Picture Library/Everett Collection; Hideo Kurihara/Alamy; LOOK Die Bildagentur der Fotografen GmbH/Alamy; Chris Fredriksson/ Alamy; Newscom; AP/Wide World Photos.

Illustration
Front Matter: John Goodwin; Kim Johnson; **U1:** QBS Learning; John Goodwin; **U2:** QBS Learning; Kim Johnson; **U3–7:** QBS Learning; **U9:** Rob Schuster; **U11–12, End Matter:** QBS Learning.

QBS Learning pp5, 16, 19, 20, 21, 23, 30, 31, 32, 36, 40, 46, 49, 50, 59, 60, 66, 69, 70, 71, 106, 110, 111, 119, 128, 130, 133, 134, 135, 140, 144

Art direction, book design, and layout services: QBS Learning
Audio production: CityVox, NYC and John Marshall Media
Video production: Steadman Productions